NEW DIRECTIONS FOR HIGHER EDUCATION

Martin Kramer
EDITOR-IN-CHIEF

Rethinking the Dissertation Process: Tackling Personal and Institutional Obstacles

Lester F. Goodchild
University of Denver

Kathy E. Green
University of Denver

Elinor L. Katz
University of Denver

Raymond C. Kluever
University of Denver

EDITORS

Number 99, Summer 1997

JOSSEY-BASS PUBLISHERS
San Francisco

RETHINKING THE DISSERTATION PROCESS: TACKLING PERSONAL AND
INSTITUTIONAL OBSTACLES
Lester F. Goodchild, Kathy E. Green, Elinor L. Katz, Raymond C. Kluever (eds.)
New Directions for Higher Education, no. 99
Volume XXV, Number 3
Martin Kramer, Editor-in-Chief

Microfilm copies of issues and articles are available in 16mm and 35mm,
as well as microfiche in 105mm, through University Microfilms Inc., 300
North Zeeb Road, Ann Arbor, Michigan 48106-1346.

ISSN 0271-0560   ISBN 0-7879-9889-3

NEW DIRECTIONS FOR HIGHER EDUCATION is part of The Jossey-Bass
Higher and Adult Education Series and is published quarterly by Jossey-
Bass Inc., Publishers, 350 Sansome Street, San Francisco, California
94104-1342. Periodicals postage paid at San Francisco, California, and at
additional mailing offices. POSTMASTER: Send address changes to New
Directions for Higher Education, Jossey-Bass Inc., Publishers, 350 Sansome Street, San Francisco, California 94104-1342.

SUBSCRIPTIONS cost $54.00 for individuals and $90.00 for institutions,
agencies, and libraries.

EDITORIAL CORRESPONDENCE should be sent to the Editor-in-Chief, Martin
Kramer, 2807 Shasta Road, Berkeley, California 94708-2011.

Cover photograph and random dot by Richard Blair/Color & Light © 1990.

Jossey-Bass Web address: http://www.josseybass.com

Printed in the United States of America on acid-free recycled paper con-
taining 100 percent recovered waste paper, of which at least 20 percent is
postconsumer waste.

CONTENTS

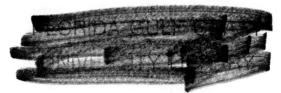

EDITORS' NOTES

The American doctoral degree has become an object of intense study, evaluation, and controversy in the past five years, receiving attention similar to that directed at both research universities and undergraduate education. Having basically maintained its original purpose and structure for the past century and a half, the Ph.D. is a tempting target for reform. Yet its central role in sustaining today's highly regarded universities and in professionalizing faculty has left many fearful of implementing any systemic change. Recent calls for reform have focused on the dissertation. This work offers a review of the personal obstacles that graduate learners face in completing this degree requirement and university efforts in assisting students to overcome them.

In 1992, Bowen and Rudenstine's *In Pursuit of the PhD* focused academics' attention on the doctoral degree across the country. They explored the issues that confronted 35,000 arts and science doctoral students from 1962 to 1986 as they sought degrees in English, history, political science, economics, mathematics, and physics. Then, in 1995, the National Research Council conducted an extensive assessment of doctoral degree programs. Opting for breadth rather than depth, it evaluated doctorates in forty-one disciplines at 274 universities, based on the assessments of approximately 7,800 faculty members (National Research Council, 1995; Webster and Skinner, 1996).

Some critics have taken a more public route. In a September 1996 *New York Times Magazine* article, Louis Menand, a CUNY faculty member, blasted the lengthy process required to obtain doctorates and suggested reforming the degree dramatically: "If all Ph.D. programs were three-year programs, with no teaching and no dissertation—if getting a doctorate were like getting a law degree—graduate education would immediately acquire focus and efficiency" (p. 81). His article drew hundreds of negative replies, with one characterizing his essay as "voodoo academic economics" ("Letters," 1996, p. 16).

A more positive discussion occurred in the *Chronicle of Higher Education,* in which Robert Atwell, the former American Council on Education president, made a plea for doctoral education to respond to "the nation's needs and the realities of the marketplace" (1996, p. B4). He called for students to do more course work and to spend less time on the dissertation. Together, all of this attention has made the doctorate a major player in the current drama on university reform.

Although doctoral programs vary across the national stage of higher education, almost all require the dissertation as a demonstration of original, creative work. The arguments against its continuation are based on its marginal utility in advancing knowledge and the negative impact it has on the cost and completion rates of doctoral programs. Doctoral education *sans* dissertation would be less expensive, less time-consuming, and altogether more sensitive to student needs as well as marketplace and academic realities. Reportedly, there is now an oversupply of doctoral students who would not be able to find jobs if they eventually finished. The dissertation is only rarely publishable without major reconstruction, often taking so long to finish that it is outdated by the time of its completion. It generally sees its greatest use collecting dust on library shelves. Furthermore, an estimated 20 to 30 percent of doctoral candidates never complete their dissertations. These abandoned educational plans waste time and money. For those desiring academic positions, the time spent in completing a dissertation may be more profitably spent in learning how to teach. Why maintain a requirement that is difficult to fulfill, leads to elusive gains for society, and causes despair for so many?

The rise of an American earned doctoral degree and research universities in the nineteenth century enabled higher education in the United States to "achieve global research leadership" (Graham and Diamond, 1997, book jacket).This development would not have occurred without the rigorous professionalization of faculty and administrators through the dissertation process. Therefore, we view the dissertation as the part of doctoral study that requires students to become independent scholars and researchers, although alternatives to the form have existed and may emerge again. For example, the dissertation may take the form of a single or several publishable articles, rather than a highly structured, lengthy volume. Writing a novel may even be appropriate. In any event, the dissertation requirement is with us, and we believe it should remain with us.

This volume addresses the condition of the dissertation and the personal and institutional factors that affect its completion. The authors represent different institutions, different positions within institutions, and different fields of study. Education is overrepresented, partly because of editor affiliation, but also because education is an area plagued by low completion rates. The charge to authors was to help us understand the complexity of the dissertation process and institutional responses to that complexity.

The first chapter describes the roles of the key players in the dissertation process: society, the university, faculty, and the student. It explores both obstacles to doctoral degree completion and possible administrative and institutional ways to resolve these problems. The second chapter chronicles the six developmental stages of the American doctorate and the dissertation. It discusses how the German research ideal, Daniel Coit Gilman at Yale and Hopkins, American research universities at the turn of the century, and accrediting associations in midcentury shaped the current form of the degree and dissertation. The next chapter discusses four methodological approaches to dissertation research and delineates the role of the dissertation chair and committee process as they assist graduate students to conduct their original research efforts. These first three chapters set the stage for the next three, which focus on student characteristics and reactions to the dissertation process.

Chapter Four explores the results of a recent study of 265 doctoral graduates and ABD students. The study shows how emotional and financial support, student research experience, and dissertation advisers' assistance, among other supports, provide necessary aids to dissertation completion. Chapter Five then examines the psychosocial factors that affect students in their efforts to complete the dissertation, with particular attention to the facets of procrastination and perfectionism. Chapter Six discusses nontraditional-aged women's experiences and the factors that enhance or inhibit their efforts to complete the dissertation. Taking the student perspective, these chapters thus address personal factors affecting doctoral completion.

The last three chapters shift to institutional patterns and support structures introduced to help students complete dissertations. Chapter Seven discusses financial and intellectual problems and support structures implemented at the University of California, Berkeley, to assist student completion of doctoral degrees. Chapter Eight reviews efforts being made in engineering and the sciences to support student completion of the dissertation, with particular attention to the needs of women and persons of color. Finally, the last chapter presents some practices that help students overcome problems in the dissertation process, with particular attention to how these may benefit th: future of doctoral study. While many other works review how to do a dissertation or describe its condition, this volume attempts to provide a broader view of the institutional and student factors affecting its completion.

Lester F. Goodchild
Kathy E. Green
Elinor L. Katz
Raymond C. Kluever

LESTER F. GOODCHILD is associate professor of education and coordinator of the Higher Education and Adult Studies Program in the College of Education at the University of Denver.

KATHY E. GREEN is professor of educational psychology in the College of Education at the University of Denver.

ELINOR L. KATZ is associate professor of education and dean of the College of Education at the University of Denver.

RAYMOND C. KLUEVER is associate professor emeritus of educational psychology in the College of Education at the University of Denver.

Society, the university, the dissertation adviser, and the candidate constitute the four key players in the dissertation process. An examination of institutional practices, dissertation obstacles, and a management system provides an analysis of this complex process.

Key Players in the Dissertation Process

Elinor L. Katz

The Doctoral Degree

The Ph.D. is the highest academic degree. According to the Council of Graduate Schools (1991), the doctoral program should prepare a student to discover, integrate, and apply knowledge, as well as disseminate and communicate it. A good graduate program develops the student's ability to contribute to the chosen field of study. A well-prepared graduate student understands and critically evaluates the literature and applies it to issues and problems. The graduate student is socialized into an academic area over a lengthy period. Whether or not the student achieves these goals depends on the key players and their roles in the process. The key players are society, the university, the dissertation adviser, and the candidate. This chapter describes each of these players.

Many doctoral students have positive and successful experiences, but a large percentage of doctoral students do not complete their degrees. Bowen and Rudenstine (1992) have examined thirty years of statistical records and report that fewer than half of all students entering Ph.D. programs finish. They note that time-to-degree (TTD) also affects completion rates. Graduate students in education have a median TTD of more than twelve years. This is one of the longest completion periods, especially compared with a typical Ph.D. recipient in the physical sciences, who completes the degree in six years.

Nerad and Cerny (1991) describe five stages of the doctoral program: (1) completing course work; (2) preparing for the oral or written qualifying exam; (3) finding a dissertation topic, selecting a dissertation adviser, and writing a proposal; (4) researching and writing the actual dissertation; and (5) applying for professional employment. Many students move through each stage successfully and with an appropriate time line. Yet, other highly qualified students experience a serious interruption in their progress. For many, this takes place at the third stage, as they enter the dissertation process.

The dissertation fulfills two major purposes. First, it is an intensive, highly professional training experience; successfully completing a dissertation demonstrates the candidate's ability to research a major intellectual problem and arrive at a successful conclusion independently and at a high level of professional competence. Second, a dissertation's results constitute an original contribution to knowledge in the field (Council of Graduate Schools, 1991). Ideally, the dissertation process is a rewarding experience for the graduate student and faculty. This volume aims to gain a better understanding of the positive and negative factors that graduate students and universities associate with completing or not completing the doctoral degree.

Many factors influence the completion or noncompletion of the doctoral degree. Completion rates and median TTD factors are two important concerns, but several other factors should also be investigated. The factors that universities could incorporate into the admitting and advising processes are of central interest.

Retaining graduate students is a major concern in higher education today. Enrollment and completion rates directly affect both a university's reputation and its financial standing. The university and students are key participants in the educational process, and a major allocation of time, energy, and resources is expected on both sides. This is especially true for the doctoral program.

The Dissertation Obstacle

The doctorate originated in medieval times. In order to teach, students needed to obtain a degree from a university. According to Cone and Foster (1993), a "sponsoring doctor" prepared graduate students for the teaching role by staying with them throughout the dissertation. This was the beginning of the dissertation committee chairperson's role. Today, the graduate student works with both a dissertation chairperson and faculty committee members, who provide support and advice throughout the dissertation process. Graduate schools require that the dissertation research proposal be approved in advance and the committee supervise this research.

Graduate study can be described as a continuum from a more structured experience during the first few years of course work to a less structured experience during the dissertation research process. Specifically, most graduate programs have two or three years of formal courses, a less defined period of requirements (such as teaching or research assignments), comprehensive examinations, and finally a less structured period of intensive dissertation research and writing (Bowen and Rudenstine, 1992). Although these aspects of the graduate program ought to be a continuous process, particular points along the way often pose problems for the graduate student.

Selecting the right dissertation topic is one of the major problems that graduate students mention. Bowen and Rudenstine (1992) state that many students spend one to two years looking for a research topic. In our University of Denver (DU) study, College of Education graduate students confirmed that selecting a topic was a major issue. They reported that they did not have enough experiences with major research projects before initiating their dissertation. Graduate students were also concerned about the work's originality, scholarly depth, and significance.

A Four-Party Process

Even though graduate students feel a sense of isolation as they write their dissertations, the dissertation experience involves society, the university, and the dissertation adviser, as well as the candidate. Each player has an important role in the successful completion of this major effort.

These four distinct parties have a vital interest in the outcome of the dissertation process. Madsen (1992) states that every time a graduate student's research sheds light on a problem, society benefits. In the United States, society foots most of the costs associated with higher education, but the research contributions are worth the costs. Every time the university grants a doctoral degree, its reputation is on the line. Society has a strong interest in maintaining the highest quality in graduate programs.

The university plays a key role in maintaining an environment that establishes high standards for graduate study. Clifford and Guthrie (1988) detail several conditions that colleges must have so that they can secure a productive role and important position in higher education. The five conditions are (1) a clear sense of organizational purpose, (2) strong leadership and competent followership, (3) effective external relationships with professional educational organizations, (4) high levels of productivity, and (5) effective alignment between organizational purposes and organizational structure.

Society, the university, and graduate programs play an important role in the completion and noncompletion of the dissertation. In a way, they create the macroenvironment of the dissertation process. On the other hand, the dissertation advisers and candidates constitute the microenvironment. According to the Council of Graduate Schools (1991), one of the dissertation adviser's major contributions is to reduce the time spent in the process and to facilitate completion of the dissertation. Advisers assist students in selecting manageable topics and in setting a realistic time line. Dissertation advisers should be actively engaged in their own advanced research and scholarship in their graduate programs.

Last but not least, the candidate is a key player. Madsen (1992) believes that the student has the most to gain from a well-written and carefully designed dissertation. The candidate can have a lasting satisfaction about having made a contribution to the field. Completion of the doctoral degree provides a sense of accomplishment and is a sign of achievement in our society.

College of Education Research Project

The DU College of Education research project, which resulted in a 1995 American Educational Research Association Symposium (Katz, Green, Kluever, Lenz, and Miller, 1995) and then this volume, concentrated on the attitudes and cognitive and affective factors influencing this process. The subjects in this study were graduate students enrolled in this midsized western university that offered a doctoral degree in education (see Chapter Four). The sample population included 154 graduates who received their degrees from 1988 to 1993. The second group included 111 students enrolled in the graduate program; having completed the comprehensive examinations, they were "All But Dissertation" (ABD) during that time. The demographics of the groups indicated the following:

1. Females made up 69 percent of the graduate group and 75 percent of the student group.
2. Males constituted 31 percent of the graduate group and 25 percent of the student group.
3. The student group (with an average age of forty-four years) was older than the graduate group (whose average age was forty-two years).
4. GRE scores were higher for the student group.
5. GPAs were similar for both groups.
6. Average time-to-degree was 6.2 years.

Overall, the two groups were more alike than different demographically.

Focus groups were used at the beginning of the study to help develop the survey. After the results were compiled, focus groups were organized to allow graduates and students to respond and react to the survey's findings. Focus groups may look like other groups, according to Krueger (1994), but focus groups have the following, distinctive set of characteristics:

1. They involve homogeneous people in a social interaction in a series of discussions.
2. Their purpose is to collect qualitative data from a structured discussion.
3. They provide a qualitative way to gather data.

Three focus groups participated in this study. In the first one, five graduates discussed their dissertation experiences and a doctoral student served as moderator. The graduates described their experiences during the dissertation process as a challenge, as a process of learning to narrow the topic until it was manageable. They reported being overwhelmed with the amount of work associated with the dissertation. What helped them complete the dissertation successfully was having supportive and encouraging advisers, remaining focused and passionate, using time management skills, and having *money*. Specific problems included time and energy, lack of guidelines, a deficit of prior research experiences, and self-discipline. Behaviors that hindered the process included delays in turning around draft copies, conflicts with or between coadvisers, and constant feelings of being overwhelmed.

The second focus group, which had eight ABD students, believed that the university should be responsible for reconnecting with and supporting doctoral students until graduation. During the dissertation process, they discovered that they had very little support after they completed course work, that dissertation courses did not help with the actual project, and that the faculty did not care if they finished. Noncompletion of the dissertation resulted from having heavy workloads, wanting to do it all and do it well, and feeling that public schools do not support the goal of completing the dissertation. If given the choice to do it over again, most said they would, but they would do it quickly, would stay in the graduate student role rather than take a full-time job, and would buy a computer. Seven off-campus students in a separate focus group said that distance from campus was an issue, as were lack of contact with faculty members and difficulty in selecting a dissertation topic.

The last focus group of six graduate students noted that family and work responsibilities were a major consideration. The group suggested that 60 percent of the problem was selecting a topic and 40 percent was selecting an adviser. Isolation from family and friends was another issue. Their best advice was to take the dissertation one step at a time and to set short-term goals.

Women and the Dissertation

Summary Report 1992: Doctorate Recipients from United States Universities (Ries and Thurgood, 1993) indicates that women continue to earn increasing numbers of doctoral degrees. In all, 14,366 women in this country have completed the Ph.D. The issues investigated in Chapter Six, entitled "Nontraditional-Aged Women and the Dissertation: A Case Study Approach," add a rich dimension to this area.

In 1996, Lenz conducted in-depth interviews with several women who completed the Ph.D. and with several ABD students. The participants from education, natural sciences, and social sciences openly discussed issues related to working on a dissertation. Recurrent themes—such as the dissertation topic and adviser, family and peer support, time, and money—confirmed the findings reported in the literature and in Kluever's and Green's survey, described respectively in Chapters Four and Five. All of the women appeared to have perfectionist tendencies, but the completers were able to move beyond the blocks and finish research projects. Another important finding involved the self-in-relation theory; completers showed more positive support from family, friends, and advisers. The completers accepted responsibility for their own dissertations. They did not expect the university or advisers to provide the motivation to complete the dissertation. One of the key factors for success with the dissertation may be internal motivation.

Barriers and Roadblocks to Completing Dissertation

Graduate students encounter barriers and roadblocks as they pursue the doctoral degree. In summarizing these obstacles, Madsen (1992) refers to ABDs as members of "The Schubert Society," because Schubert composed the "Unfinished Symphony." Many factors influence the completion or noncompletion of the dissertation, including a shortage of money, illness, marital discord, and other personal problems that interfere with the research project. With regard to the dissertation, the topic becomes unmanageable, enthusiasm wanes, and time slips away. Madsen (1992) considers five of the circumstances that cause delays in the dissertation process.

Too Early a Departure. The best advice for doctoral students is to stay on campus until the dissertation is finished or not to leave the university without the degree in hand. Too many times, economic pressures and the enticement of a wonderful job opportunity pull the doctoral student away from campus. Once away from academic life, the student has too little time or energy to work on the dissertation. If a student needs to leave campus, the second best advice is to have as much of the dissertation completed as possible before departing.

Too Much Enthusiasm, Too Little Focus. Graduate students have a tendency to be interested in and enthusiastic about many topics. They bring a great deal of energy to the research project. The challenge is to narrow the scope of their interests so that they can select a topic and establish a reasonable time line.

Too Hard to Please. Some students never complete the dissertation because there is one more citation, another section for the literature review, more examples of research studies, and so forth, until time moves on and the student puts the dissertation on the shelf. The perfectionist requires support, understanding, and agreed-upon deadlines. An adviser can play an important part in helping the student set realistic goals and schedules.

Too Long in Transit. A fear of failure or fear of success increases the time involved in working on the dissertation. Working on a research or writing project tends to bring out the procrastinator in all of us. If students cannot come to grips with this issue, they remain in transit for long periods.

Too Much Isolation. For many students, working on the dissertation is a lonely and isolated experience. The long hours spent looking for sources in the library, reading research materials, and writing the dissertation separate the doctoral student from activities with family and friends. Few experiences in life isolate people from each other for such an extended period.

Doctoral students have vested interests in successfully completing their dissertations. "Every time a graduate student's dissertation sheds some light on a dark corner of human understanding and banishes some segment, however small of the world's mystery, society reaps incalculable benefits" (Madsen, 1992, p. 14). The challenge for graduate programs is to understand the barriers and roadblocks and to use them to analyze current policies and practices.

That way, a student might feel more supported and the dissertation process might be more effective for both the faculty adviser and candidate.

A Management System for Doctoral Students

There are many ways to improve the dissertation process. Students may have difficulty shifting from a structured environment of course work, papers, and defined assignments to an environment that lacks a defined structure and specific time line. Students need many different skills to complete the dissertation successfully. They must be able to write well, manage time, and make a plan for completing the dissertation. Students should create their own comprehensive management system. It begins when the doctoral student enters the graduate program, designs a course work plan that includes research skills and experiences, develops a dissertation proposal, implements the dissertation research, and successfully defends the dissertation study. Students can easily follow the five steps outlined in this section.

Step 1: Preparation for Research. The doctoral degree is designed as a research program in which a student's research knowledge and experience are the keys to success. A university program should provide the courses and research experiences needed to guide the student through the process. Research projects and studies need to be integrated into the whole doctoral program. It is highly recommended that social science students have a knowledge of both quantitative and qualitative approaches to research.

Step 2: Graduate Program Design. By the time students are accepted into a doctoral program, they have successfully completed a great deal of academic work. Yet many students come into the doctoral program with only minimal research skills. Students should be encouraged to seek out research projects from the beginning of the doctoral degree. They should take courses that build research skills and assist in the development of a dissertation proposal. A sample research course sequence developed for a college of education on a quarter system appears in Figure 1.1. Foundation requirements prepare students for more advanced methods and courses. Dissertation seminars or research practica then give students experience in writing research proposals and conducting studies. The intent of dissertation seminars and research practica is to compel students to integrate skills acquired in methods courses.

Step 3: Proposal Development. Students have more questions than answers at the beginning of the dissertation. Here is a sample of the questions they ask and the answers they receive: "Question: What are the quality standards? Answer: High! Question: How long should a dissertation be? Answer: Long enough to cover the topic. Question: How exhaustive should the literature review be? Answer: Exhaustive" (Davis and Parker, 1979, p. 35). Students cannot define the scope of the dissertation easily. They need adequate time to determine the topic, select the adviser and committee members, and develop the proposal. In the proposal, they also need to lay out a detailed plan for

Figure 1.1. The DU College of Education
Ph.D. Research Course Sequence

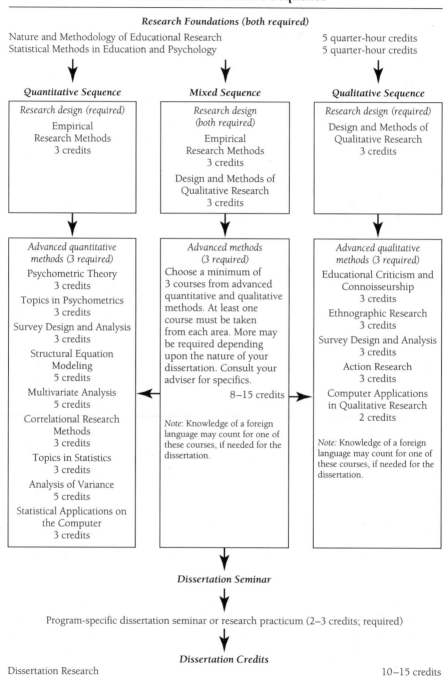

Research Foundations (both required)

Nature and Methodology of Educational Research	5 quarter-hour credits
Statistical Methods in Education and Psychology	5 quarter-hour credits

Quantitative Sequence	*Mixed Sequence*	*Qualitative Sequence*
Research design (required) Empirical Research Methods 3 credits	*Research design* *(both required)* Empirical Research Methods 3 credits Design and Methods of Qualitative Research 3 credits	*Research design (required)* Design and Methods of Qualitative Research 3 credits
Advanced quantitative *methods (3 required)* Psychometric Theory 3 credits Topics in Psychometrics 3 credits Survey Design and Analysis 3 credits Structural Equation Modeling 5 credits Multivariate Analysis 5 credits Correlational Research Methods 3 credits Topics in Statistics 3 credits Analysis of Variance 5 credits Statistical Applications on the Computer 3 credits	*Advanced methods* *(3 required)* Choose a minimum of 3 courses from advanced quantitative and qualitative methods. At least one course must be taken from each area. More may be required depending upon the nature of your dissertation. Consult your adviser for specifics. 8–15 credits *Note:* Knowledge of a foreign language may count for one of these courses, if needed for the dissertation.	*Advanced qualitative* *methods (3 required)* Educational Criticism and Connoisseurship 3 credits Ethnographic Research 3 credits Survey Design and Analysis 3 credits Action Research 3 credits Computer Applications in Qualitative Research 2 credits *Note:* Knowledge of a foreign language may count for one of these courses, if needed for the dissertation.

Dissertation Seminar

Program-specific dissertation seminar or research practicum (2–3 credits; required)

Dissertation Credits

Dissertation Research	10–15 credits

researching and writing the dissertation. Many students find that writing the proposal is the most time-consuming phase in the process.

Step 4: Dissertation Research. Once the proposal is approved, the work begins. Managing the project—especially writing, gathering data, and analyzing results—can be the greatest challenges of the dissertation. Students complain of "drowning in the data" or "feeling isolated and alone" during this stage of the research project. Having a planned strategy is crucial at this time. Students should consider the following steps:

1. Make sure the writing is clear and concise.
2. Understand the relationship between the research questions and methodology.
3. Have access to a computer and the software needed for the study.
4. Develop a time management plan and plan to revise it often.
5. Know the university's guidelines for dissertations.

Even if students have detailed plans for the dissertation process, they need to plan for the unexpected. Cone and Foster (1993) suggest that students examine their "cognitive ecology." They cite Mahoney and Mahoney (1976), who coined this term to describe a process of weeding out irrational thinking. For example, it is irrational to assume that the dissertation process will run smoothly. It is irrational when students set out to create the definitive study on a topic. With this line of thinking, the student may never finish the dissertation. Perfectionist tendencies can pose a serious problem for doctoral students. The best advice is to set realistic expectations and goals for the study. The dissertation is the beginning of a long line of research experiences.

Step 5: Dissertation Defense. The student completes the dissertation process by defending the research study before a faculty committee. Students are well advised to prepare for this event, even if they know a great deal about the topic and design. Each university has a procedure and a long tradition of how the oral defense is conducted. Students should learn how long the orals take, how much time students can take to summarize the study, which types of audiovisual aids are allowed, and what kinds of questions have been asked at previous oral examinations. Doing a "walk through" of the orals with an adviser is highly recommended.

Improving the Dissertation Process

The four key players in the dissertation process can benefit from considering recommendations that would lead to successful completion of the doctoral degree. Bernard Berelson's *Graduate Education in the United States* (1960) still has several important ideas about this matter. He suggests (1) doing doctoral studies for no longer than four years, (2) having better faculty advising, (3) shortening dissertations, (4) regularizing postdoctoral study, (5) freeing departments to determine language requirements, (6) eliminating the oral examination, (7) having students pay more of the costs of doctoral education, (8) gaining greater assistance from multiple sources in helping ABDs complete their degrees, and (9) finding greater corporate support for doctoral research. Concerning students, he recommends (1) seeking better admissions advising regarding graduate degrees, (2) receiving assistance earlier in overcoming writing difficulties, and (3) seeking research opportunities (pp. 234–248).

Since Berelson proposed these changes, many people have revised them. The most promising suggestions include (1) decreasing the number of admissions into doctoral programs (Noble, 1994; Snell, 1963); (2) providing greater financial assistance to students, especially those who are completing their dissertations (Bowen and Rudenstine, 1992; Noble, 1994); (3) shortening the length of doctoral study (Bowen and Rudenstine, 1992); (4) "restricting the dissertation somewhat in scope of topic, amount of research expected or length" (Atwell, 1996; Snell, 1963); (5) creating dissertation workshops to facilitate student progress (Bowen and Rudenstine, 1992); and (6) providing better training for future teaching (Atwell, 1996; Carmichael, 1961). After having examined some recommendations for students, this chapter now explores some specific recommendations for the other three players.

Society. In many fields of study society needs highly trained specialists. The current number or quality of doctoral students cannot satisfy this need. To meet increasing demands, we need to attract more graduate students and shepherd them through graduate school more efficiently (Ziolkowski, 1990). Other studies, however, indicate that an oversupply of Ph.D.'s in such fields as English, history, and physics are seeking positions in university settings. Society must decide how to support the research and applications needed to advance our culture and how to balance that with professional positions for new graduates.

University. The university should provide a well-organized academic program with clearly defined expectations for graduate students. Faculty members should consider themselves to be a community of scholars and should reflect this behavior in research and teaching activities. Universities need to provide students with financial aid during their dissertation research. A graduate program could reserve a number of graduate student assistantships or doctoral fellowships for students actively engaged in their research project.

Graduate programs should do a program review of the research course and practicum offerings to see if the courses provide the skills needed to conduct dissertation research. Members of the faculty and graduates of the doctoral program should participate in this review process. Upon entering a doctoral program, students should receive information about the program's research expectations. Faculty members should reinforce the expectation of research throughout the course work by requiring independent research projects, supporting students who present conference papers, and holding research days in which faculty and students present their work to others in the department or in the university.

Graduate programs should annually update a list of graduate students, their dissertation faculty advisers, and their research topics, providing that list to departmental faculty and administrators. Students should have access to a similar list that indicates faculty members' areas of research, publications, and availability to advise a dissertation. A dissertation handbook with details about standard expectations for both graduate students and advisers would be most useful. It is also important for graduate programs to keep records about the length of time each student takes to complete the doctoral dissertation (Council of Graduate Schools, 1991).

Dissertation Advisers. Doctoral students look to dissertation advisers to be role models and support systems. An adviser can help graduate students select manageable topics, define the scope of the research, help with time management, and encourage completion of the dissertation (Council of Graduate Schools, 1991). The university could match entering students with advisers based on interests and personality.

Dissertation advisers should consider organizing dissertation support groups, seminars, or a Dissertation Day. The University of Denver has sponsored informal support groups, monthly seminars, and a Dissertation Day for students who have left campus. Advisers can also team students who are at the same point in the process; teams can provide mutual support. A supportive environment helps students complete the dissertation and reduces their sense of isolation.

For example, a university offered two workshops to graduate students working on their dissertations. The topics were "Practical Strategies for Writing a Dissertation" and "The View from the Other Side of the Desk" (Nerad and Cerny, 1991). The second seminar's purpose is to have advisers describe their expectations for the dissertation. Other interesting topics to discuss are creating time management strategies, balancing personal and professional responsibilities while working on the dissertation, and using technology in research projects.

It is important to remember that the dissertation is the beginning of one's scholarly work, not the culmination. Dissertation research should prepare students for the research or scholarship that will be expected after they receive their degrees (Council of Graduate Schools, 1991).

Chapter Six of this volume provides many recommendations for completing a dissertation. Several graduates share advice with students struggling with the dissertation. The graduates suggest that the dissertation process is more about the student and his or her personal growth, professional skills, and attitude than about external factors, such as advisers, topics, data, and university requirements. These aspects of graduate education serve as opportunities for students to become more self-actualized persons and more competent professionals.

The graduates also recommend that the students love their topics passionately. Students should contribute to the body of knowledge in their field. They must make a time line and stick with it. They should make good use of their committees by having monthly meetings and sticking to a schedule. Students should make sure that their accomplishments satisfy their promises to their advisers. Students should learn to eat the elephant one bite at a time.

Examining the roles of the key players reveals the connections that must exist so that a student can successfully complete the dissertation. We need to examine many factors so that we can understand the issues better. The succeeding chapters in this volume reflect our understanding of some of these factors.

ELINOR L. KATZ is associate professor of education and dean of the College of Education at the University of Denver.

uate courses, separate from baccalaureate studies. Students were required [to h]ave completed a bachelor's degree before beginning these courses. More-[over], they had to reside at the college until they finished their course work. [Alth]ough graduate enrollments varied over the next thirty years, a separate [grad]uate department of philosophy and arts was created in 1847 (Storr, 1953, [pp.]54–56). In the same year, two well-known science professors, John P. Nor-[ton] and Benjamin Silliman, Jr., established the Scientific School, a laboratory [of s]cientific research (Cordasco, 1973, p. 19). This postbaccalaureate school [offe]red liberal arts and science courses in "chemistry, mineralogy, geology, [bota]ny, mathematics, physics, meteorology, and astronomy" (Gilman, 1898, [pp.]125, 131). In both units, American doctoral education began.

The First Doctorate. Yale's earned doctoral studies came into existence [thro]ugh the influence of Daniel Coit Gilman (1831–1908). After graduating [from] Yale in 1852 with a bachelor's degree, Gilman spent the next summer [stud]ying at Harvard. During the following two years, he attended lectures and [sem]inars at German universities and at scientific schools. Gilman then returned [to Y]ale, where he helped develop a new plan for the renamed Sheffield Scien-[tific] School at the invitation of Professor James D. Dana. In 1856, Gilman pub-[lish]ed a *Proposed Plan for a Complete Organization of the School of Science [Con]nected with Yale College*. In this plan, he called for the creation of a doctor [of p]hilosophy degree, which was to be awarded after a rigorous examination. [Alth]ough Gilman acknowledged the educational practices and influences of [othe]r countries on this proposed degree, he believed it was most important "to [ada]pt them to local conditions and to the wants of America" (Cordasco, 1973, [pp.]3, 24–26). Others would take this plan one step further.

In July 1860, John A. Porter, dean of the Sheffield Scientific School, peti-[tion]ed the president and fellows of Yale to allow both the school and the [Dep]artment of Philosophy and Arts to offer a doctoral degree "in accordance [wit]h the usage of German universities." Students were expected to undertake [two] years of graduate study, achieve proficiency in languages (Greek and Latin [in t]he department or French or German in the school), pass an examination [on]their studies, and complete a thesis. In regard to this last requirement, [Por]ter stated that the thesis "shall be approved by the faculty giving the results [of a]n *original* chemical or physical investigation" (italics added, Cordasco, [197]3, pp. 28–29; Storr, 1953, p. 57).

With its clear link to German doctoral education, Porter's request points [to t]he adoption of the *Wissenschaft* ideal of original research for the American [deg]ree. The Yale trustees approved the granting of the degree in the same year. [In 1]861, the college awarded it to three students who achieved this "high [sta]ndard of attainments" (Gilman, 1898, pp. 134–135). Yale had determined [the]basic requirements for the American earned doctoral degree: discrete [stu]dy, languages, an examination, and a thesis. Gilman thus played a pivotal [par]t in America's first earned doctorate. Later, Harvard's president Charles W. [Elio]t acknowledged and praised Gilman's role for "introducing a good Ph.D. [int]o the United States" (Eliot, 1897). Between 1870 and 1889, Pennsylvania,

Aspirations to advance knowledge led nineteenth-century American educators to create doctoral degrees and to found research universities. The original rationale for the doctorate was to teach graduate students who had an academic vocation how to conduct pure and applied research. The doctorate's 141-year-old degree requirements have remained substantially the same.

The American Doctorate and Dissertation: Six Developmental Stages

Lester F. Goodchild, Margaret M. Miller

American research universities play a crucial role in contemporary North American society. "They conduct about half of the basic research in the United States, train almost all the Ph.D.s and medical doctors, and also graduate about 30 percent of the country's bachelors. They have been heralded as central institutions of post-industrial societies, although other advanced countries have nothing that equals them. . . . They stand alone in the world in terms of their abundant numbers, variety of their forms, and the extent to which they derive their sustenance from numerous sources" (Geiger, 1993, p. vii). They were differentiated from other institutions of higher learning or scientific institutes when the doctorate emerged in the mid-nineteenth-century United States. Graduate students sought this degree as professional training for the academic life of teaching and inquiry. Therefore, the mission of American research universities subsists in the vitality of the doctorate.

As the quintessential mission of these new universities, research gained prominence over other purposes and functions during the past century and a half. One may discern its link to a formal degree and thesis as early as Daniel Coit Gilman's efforts to introduce an earned doctorate at Yale in 1856 (Cordasco, 1973, p. 25). Six developmental stages in the evolution of the doctor of philosophy degree have produced its contemporary structure. This degree's advancement, driven by the demand for new knowledge and the necessary creation of related institutional structures, shaped the American higher education system. According to the Carnegie Foundation for the Advancement of Teaching's classification (1994), now 125 top research universities award the most prestigious doctoral degrees. In 1994, a total of four hundred universities awarded 43,863 doctorates (*Digest of Education Statistics,* 1996). These developments have often been portrayed in idealistic accounts. Actually, this achievement would not have occurred if individuals, groups, and organizations had not continually and contentiously struggled to promote, enhance, and reform the degree's role in the rise of American science and the professionalization of the academic vocation.

This chapter offers a new historical overview of the development of this degree and the dissertation, paying particular attention to the difficulties encountered in this process as well as to student reactions. It covers the two major eras in the degree's evolution, which collectively comprise six developmental stages. In the formative era from 1787 to 1899, American educators sought to create earned doctorates and research universities. Within this era, two distinct stages may be perceived. First, from 1787 to 1874, graduate education and the earned doctorate began. Second, from 1875 to 1899, American research universities were established, and all doctoral degrees became tied to original research.

In the expansive era from 1900 to the present, the growth of doctoral programs at many universities next provided greater opportunities for students to enter the academic profession. One can perceive three distinct and one overlapping stage in which struggles to maintain quality, multiplication, and periodic assessments took place. First, from 1900 to 1937, the Association of American Universities (AAU) played a standardizing role to ensure the doctorate's quality. Second, from 1938 to 1957, regional accrediting associations allowed a greater number of universities to offer the doctorate. Third, from 1958 to the present, doctoral research and education received federal funding as national defense, health, and science priorities. Fourth, from 1960 to the present, doctoral education received extensive scrutiny. Thus, this chapter provides a foundational overview for this volume on the current status of the dissertation as well as the personal and institutional factors affecting its completion.

The Emergence of Graduate Education and Earned Doctoral Studies, 1787 to 1874

After the American Revolution, the need for graduate education and universities arose, as four developments reflect. First, a federal mandate to develop universities began in 1787 when the Constitutional Convention called for a national university. Although the country's first six presidents supported this idea, it never resulted in the founding of an institution (Brubacher and Rudy, 1968, p. 225). Not until 1862 did the Morrill Land-Grant Act provide the legislative vehicle for federal sponsorship of state universities. Subsequent congressional actions enhanced the relationship between the federal government and public colleges and universities. First, the 1887 Hatch Act provided funding for "agricultural experiment stations" that enabled land-grant university faculty to offer farmers better advice on their crops. Second, the 1890 Morrill Land-Grant Act created land-grant universities for African Americans in the South as well as "annual federal appropriations for general academic programs" for all such institutions.

These federal laws occurred because of the intense lobbying [of Penn]sylvania State College president George W. Atherton and othe[rs] ers who secured the distinctive role that the federal governm[ent has in] funding higher education (Williams, 1991, p. 3). In retros[pect, this] state partnership provided the rationale and funding for a [number] of state universities, which would eventually include gradua[te programs].

Second, the model for such state universities came from [Virginia. Its] president Thomas Jefferson and Charles Fenton Mercer, a me[mber of the] House of Delegates, championed the new university "as a gra[duate school"] in 1825, comparable with others in Europe (Storr, 1953, p[p. ...]. [Although] their graduate intention went unrealized, although their crea[tion of] sep- arate schools of study, which had Scottish roots (Sloan, 197[1, ...] became an important addition to the developing American [university]. This programmatic structure thus presaged the future depar[tments of] academic study, which encouraged the development of gra[duate education]. Still, something more was needed.

Two other forces that provided a distinctive raison d'être [came] from Europe. One represented the German university, and t[he other embod]ied American students' experience of it. Beginning in 1810, [the University of] Berlin offered a new model of research. *Wissenschaft* exemp[lified this] approach to the study of phenomena. It combined a critical a[ttitude and a] "balanced concern for both scientific facts and human values[" (Ben-David,] p. 57). In humanistic studies, this approach was more philos[ophical, entail]ing a critical method of investigation (Veysey, 1965, pp. [...]. These approaches encouraged professors and students to explore k[nowledge for its] own sake, usually without any explicitly utilitarian conside[rations. Between] 1820 and 1920, approximately nine thousand American stu[dents studied in] Germany. Doctoral education at German universities provided [a rigorous train]ing experience unavailable in the United States and difficul[t to obtain else]where. Matriculation for the German degree was readily ha[d, and requirements] were straightforward; they included "successful attendance a[t lectures for as] little as two years, an acceptable thesis, and the passing of a[n] oral examination" (Herbst, 1965, pp. 1, 9).

These heady encounters left returning Americans eager t[o introduce gradu]ate education at the few institutions where it was offered. [While George] Ticknor's curricular reforms at Harvard failed, Henry Philip Tap[pan did] better at the University of Michigan, where he instituted lectu[res and] concentrations (Storr, 1953; Turner and Bernard, 1989). Grea[ter change would] occur when academic leaders sought to replicate their foreign [experiences] in the United States, tailoring them to American practices and [offering them] at new universities for those unable or unwilling to travel to [Europe. These] four forces thus shaped the development of American graduate [education dur]ing the nineteenth century.

Early Graduate Studies. Founded in 1701, Yale figures [prominently in] the beginnings of graduate education. As early as 1814, faculty [members]

Harvard, Columbia, Princeton, and Brown also matched this graduate effort in that order (Cordasco, 1973, p. 16, n. 5). Yet a larger step was needed. Gilman would create a different type of institution to take the degree to its next developmental stage.

The First American Research Universities and the Dissertation, 1875 to 1899

The rise of research universities created an institutional mission particularly devoted to research. During most of the nineteenth century, American college presidents' focus on traditional undergraduate education had hampered early efforts at expanding graduate education. New universities displaced this inhibition by seeking greater advancement of knowledge through research, especially in the sciences. This effort finally succeeded in 1875 because of Gilman's efforts at Johns Hopkins University. It influenced the subsequent establishments of Clark University, Catholic University of America, and the University of Chicago—to name only the first of such new institutions. Their doctoral productivity, regulations, and student reactions reflected a new prospect for higher learning.

Gilman and Johns Hopkins University. Leaving New Haven because of President Noah Porter's antipathy toward graduate education (Cordasco, 1973, pp. 32–33), Gilman assumed the presidency in 1872 of the new land-grant University of California. For the next three years, he endeavored to create not another Berlin or Yale but an institution, in an often-repeated ideal, that "must be adapted to this people, to their public and private schools, to their peculiar geographical position, to the requirements of their new society and their undeveloped resources" (Gilman, 1898, p. 157).

While Gilman struggled to develop this institution, he received a more attractive call to found a major university from back East. In November 1874, the trustees of Johns Hopkins University, with the backing of its founder's $3.5 million, inquired about Gilman's interest in becoming the new president of Johns Hopkins University. There he could blend his desire to expand graduate education with his determination to Americanize its structure. Gilman offered the trustees a new research ideal in which the "promotion of advanced scholarship and training of graduate students would be his aims in the new university" (Hawkins, 1960, pp. 3, 21–22). In his formal acceptance in January 1875, Gilman added "the promotion of Christian civilization" to the university's mission (Gilman, 1875; Marsden, 1994).

Before taking up his duties in Baltimore, Gilman visited many European institutions of higher learning. He went to the leading German universities of Berlin and Leipzig to assess scientific education, especially chemistry and physics laboratories as well as schools of medicine (Gilman, 1875). When he established himself at Hopkins, various pressures from trustees and the local community required Gilman to include undergraduate studies. Nevertheless, the graduate orientation remained the university's strongest feature (Hawkins, 1960, pp. 27–28).

The Research University's Mission. Gilman's inaugural address on February 22, 1876, described the new American research university mission. Although these universities owed much to European institutions, Gilman hoped that they would maintain certain values, practices, and traditions that were part of American higher education. He believed that they should do more than create "learned pedants, simple artisans, or cunning sophists, or pretentious practitioners." Rather "the object of the university was to develop character . . . not so much to impart knowledge to pupils, as to whet the appetite, exhibit methods, develop powers, strengthen judgment, and invigorate the intellectual and moral forces" (1898, pp. 19–20). Later, at a Phi Beta Kappa speech given at Harvard, Gilman would point out "the development of talent" as one of the university's most important goals. Others included "the advancement of learning, the conservation of knowledge, . . . the promotion of spirituality, the cultivation of literature, the elevation of professional standards, and the maintenance of repose" (1886, pp. 27–28). Although the university mission was devoted to research (Gilman, 1898, p. 296; Veysey, 1965, pp. 160–165), it continued the unique American educational objective of combining teaching with a focus on student talent and character development within a Christian context. This mission was thus derived in part from the country's 250-year-old college tradition.

Doctoral Degree Requirements. Universities encouraged the development of future scholars and researchers through many approaches. Initially, lectures and seminars at Hopkins provided the means of imparting knowledge and developing skills. Moreover, twenty fellowships allowed students the opportunity to study full-time (Storr, 1973, pp. 41–43; *Johns Hopkins University Register,* 1877–1878, p. 26). During the required two-year instructional period in one of its departments, students demonstrated their growing professional expertise through "written, oral, or practical" examinations.

These academic achievements prepared graduate students for undertaking the most demanding next step in the doctoral process. Successfully completing and defending the dissertation demonstrated professional academic competence. As the research university developed, dissertation requirements became more formal. Yet the demand for originality was straightforward from the beginning. The published thesis requirements were clear: students had "to produce a thesis which shall be approved by the Faculty. This thesis must be the result of original investigation in the main subject for examination, and the subject of the thesis must be submitted for approval to the head of the department, or the chief examiner in it, not less than six months before the degree is conferred" (*Johns Hopkins University Register,* 1877–1878, p. 25). Students also had to undertake investigations in their theses that showed methodological expertise. As Hopkins chemists noted during that first year, the "dissertation . . . shall be, not a mere compilation, such as could be worked up in a good library, but a discussion of some problem on the basis of experiments undertaken by the candidate for the purpose of solving the problem. The discipline attendant upon this work will lead him to see by what means the science has been built up, and his interest will be awakened in the work done" (Hawkins, 1960, pp. 223–224).

In 1878, Gilman put these requirements more formally in his annual report to the trustees. The candidate, Gilman wrote, should demonstrate "mastery of his subject, his powers of independent thought as well as of careful research, and his ability to express, in a clear and systematic order, and in appropriate language, the results of his study" (Hawkins, 1960, p. 123). The administration later added other requirements to the dissertation and the reception of the doctorate. Pressure for more time to be given to learning and research led the administration to demand in 1881 that students spend three years between receiving their baccalaureate degrees and their doctorates. Faculty also expected students to publish their thesis or dissertation in the growing number of research journals that Hopkins and other universities or professional academic associations sponsored. Furthermore, the university administration began requiring students in 1884 to print 150 copies of their theses at their own expense (Hawkins, 1960, pp. 75, 109, 123–124). These copies were sent to other university and college libraries across the country, adding to the prestige of the individual and the university. Administrators wanted this new knowledge to be shared among professional colleagues. Successful completion of these requirements by men initially and women after 1907 led to the conferral of the doctor of philosophy degree. (After this date, women also became eligible to receive Ph.D.'s at Hopkins, which was still behind Yale, Chicago, and Clark universities, where women already were being admitted to graduate studies [Gordon, 1990; Koelsch, 1987, pp. 72–74].) Hopkins's requirements soon became the model that all other universities embraced (Geiger, 1986, pp. 8–9).

Thus Gilman's design for Johns Hopkins University focused not only on producing new knowledge but also on creating an institution in which both the liberal arts and science contributed to its being "the most potent of all agencies for the advancement and promulgation of learning" (Gilman, 1898, p. 48). The president had combined many European and American traditions to devise this new university mission that emphasized developing *Wissenschaft* scholars. Gilman had wanted to create this type of American university from his earliest postbaccalaureate days. In an April 1876 letter to Professor Dana at Yale, Gilman indicated that their first discussions on how to develop the Scientific School twenty years previously had been crucial to his vision and plans for the new university (Cordasco, 1973, p. 67, n. 4; Gilman, 1898, pp. 146–147).

Students' Reactions to Doctoral Study. The development of research skills and professional expertise did not always come easily. Abraham Flexner and Woodrow Wilson were two major figures in American higher education who reacted differently to the Hopkins setting. When Flexner attended the university as a seventeen-year-old undergraduate in 1884, he noted that "research was in the air we breathed" at the Johns Hopkins (1940, p. 57). He had high praise for Hopkins's president Daniel Coit Gilman and noted that undergraduate and graduate students were treated similarly. Flexner became one of the great reformers of American medical education and universities.

At the same time, Woodrow Wilson worked toward his doctoral degree in history at Johns Hopkins. Although he questioned the lecturing of Professor Adams, he agreed with Flexner in his overall sentiment. Wilson was happy to attend the university, because he believed that Johns Hopkins was the best in the United States. He lamented, however, that his department (history and politics) was "weakly manned as regards its corps of instructors. . . . Of our three Ph.D.'s, one is insincere and superficial, the second a man stuffed full of information but apparently much too full to have any movement which is not an impulse from somebody else, and the third merely a satellite of the first." Like many students, Wilson disliked lectures from most faculty: "One of the wags of our class suggested that the lectures to which we are daily invited were intended for our recreation, as agreeable interruptions to our severer studies" (1966, vol. 2, p. 552). Yet G. Stanley Hall stood out among his professors: "I attend not only because I am to be a pedagogue, but because I find Dr. Hall one of the most interesting and suggestive men [at] the 'Varsity. He is full of ideas and has a pleasant, straightforward, man-of-the-world's way of imparting them" (Wilson, 1966, vol. 3, p. 430). Wilson also disliked and expressed boredom with "cramming for examination." He entertained notions about not completing his Ph.D. (1966, vol. 3, pp. 379, 414–415), primarily because the department did not closely match his interests in political science. Nevertheless, Wilson completed his doctorate and later became the president of Princeton and then the United States.

Other Research Universities. While Yale and Harvard continued to expand their doctoral offerings, Clark University and Catholic University of America opened as solely graduate institutions in 1889. After leaving Johns Hopkins University, where he had been professor of psychology and pedagogy, G. Stanley Hall became the president of Clark and launched the institution, with the benefactor's $1 million. Fifteen Hopkins faculty joined him in Massachusetts (Goodchild, 1996; Koelsch, 1987). Meanwhile, Catholic University also adopted this research mission with only a $300,000 founding gift. Unfortunately, a financial disaster involving the endowment in 1904 curtailed its fiscal vitality and the extent of its doctoral education in comparison with other research universities (Nuesse, 1990). Each university eventually accommodated undergraduate students because of continuing financial difficulties or better prospects of financial stability. Within ten years after Clark and Catholic universities opened, however, their administrations and faculty were forced to focus more on research and study related to psychology and theology, respectively (Veysey, 1965).

In 1892, another major research university was established that could claim to embody, if not surpass, Hopkins's ideals and mission. John D. Rockefeller gave $35 million to create the University of Chicago (Goodspeed, 1916, p. 293). President William Rainey Harper began the university with 120 faculty members to carry on the new American research ethos in the Midwest, including half of the faculty raided from Clark University (Geiger, 1986, p. 11; Koelsch, 1987).

Table 2.1. Total Number of Doctorates Awarded at Hopkins, Clark, Catholic, and Chicago During Their First Twenty-Five Years, 1878 to 1919

Division/Discipline	Hopkins[a] 1878–1903 # (% of Total Doctorates)	Clark[b] 1891–1916 # (% of Total Doctorates)	Catholic[c] 1894–1919 # (% of Total Doctorates)	Chicago[d] 1893–1918 # (% of Total Doctorates)	Total Number of Doctorates
Sciences					
Animal Physiology	18	0	0	0	18
Astronomy	5	0	0	16	21
Biology/Zoology	35	10	2	55	102
Botany	3	0	0	106	109
Chemistry	125	5	7	101	238
Geography	0	0	0	6	6
Geology	27	0	0	50	77
Home Economics	0	0	0	3	3
Hygiene and Bacteriology	0	0	0	6	6
Mathematics	36	18	1	84	139
Pathology	1	0	0	17	18
Physics	51	18	0	50	119
Physiology	6	0	0	40	46
Psychology	2	88	4	39	133
Subtotal	309 (50)	139 (80)	14 (20)	573 (54)	1,035 (54)
Humanities					
Art	0	0	0	1	1
Comparative religions	0	0	0	3	3
English	37	0	10	48	95
German languages	15	0	0	49	98
Greek	55	0	2	41	64
History	115	8	0	54	177
Latin	26	0	6	33	65
New Testament	0	0	0	33	33
Oriental languages	0	0	0	42	42
Philology	0	0	0	10	10
Philosophy	9	0	9	48	66
Romance languages	38	0	0	20	58
Sanskrit	7	0	0	0	7
Semiotics	11	0	0	0	11
Theology	0	0	14	0	14
Subtotal	313 (50)	8 (4.5)	41 (59)	382 (36)	744 (38)
Social sciences					
Anthropology	0	3	0	0	3
Economics	0	0	0	33	33
Education	0	22	9	26	57
Political Science	0	0	6	12	18
Sociology	0	2	0	38	40
Subtotal	0 (0)	27 (15.5)	15 (21)	109 (10)	151 (8)
Total	622 (100)	174 (100)	70 (100)	1,064 (100)	1,930 (100)

(a) Johns Hopkins Library, 1926.
(b) Corrected copy of dissertation list, Goddard Library, Clark University, 1991.
(c) Commencement Bulletins, 1894–1919, Catholic University of America. Record of only Ph.D.'s, not Roman pontifical degrees.
(d) University of Chicago Announcements, 1931.

Of the four new research universities, Hopkins became the institutional progenitor for an American research ideal now anchored to an earned doctoral degree. The new standard included successful completion of graduate courses and seminars, language examinations, comprehensive written and oral examinations, and a dissertation that reflected original research.

Doctoral Productivity at Hopkins, Clark, Catholic, and Chicago. The first twenty-five years of doctoral productivity at Hopkins, Clark, Catholic, and Chicago pointed to the predominance of science research (see Table 2.1). Of the 1,930 dissertations written at these institutions during those years, 1,035, or 54 percent, were in the natural and biological sciences. As the number of awarded doctorates show, certain disciplines stood out at all four institutions as most attractive to students. Responding to the demands of an industrializing American society, students wrote dissertations in the following fields: chemistry (238), mathematics (139), physics (119), biology/zoology (102), and geology (77). President Hall of Clark University, who was one of the country's leading psychologists and who founded the American Psychological Association, attracted many students as psychology developed and expanded during this period. Of the 133 psychology doctorates awarded at these universities, 88 came from Clark.

Similar to the sciences, doctoral production in other disciplines and developing fields depended often on leading scholars who were creating these new knowledge domains. In the humanities, history (177) stood out above all, because of the famous work of Hopkins's Herbert Baxter Adams, who founded the American Historical Association. Most students in the humanities took languages in preparation for future college academic positions: Greek (98), English (95), Latin (65), and Romance languages (58). Clearly, the social sciences were just developing as fields of study; education (57) and sociology (40) were significantly attractive in this developing Progressive Era.

Most of these early dissertations were written as articles to be published in journals. Therefore, they tended to be shorter and did not have the extensive literature reviews common today. Longer works were published as books, however. The requirement that dissertations be printed lasted until the 1920s, when typescript dissertations became acceptable. Thereafter, their length increased, although this tended to vary by discipline (see Berelson, 1960, p. 181, for median page lengths during this period).

This analysis provides only a limited picture of doctoral productivity across the forty-eight universities offering the doctorate by 1900 (Hawkins, 1992, pp. 11–12). Nonetheless, it shows the significant doctoral production at three leading new research universities.

The New Era of Doctoral Expansion in the Twentieth Century

Having explored in great depth the formative era of the American doctorate, this chapter now examines the expansion of the doctorate. This section offers shorter summaries of the remaining four developmental periods, saving greater analysis for a later work.

Standardization Through the AAU, 1900 to 1937. In 1900, Hopkins, Clark, Catholic, Chicago, and ten other charter institutions formed the prestigious Association of American Universities. This organization controlled the quality of doctoral programs until just after the Second World War. The development of professional associations and institutional consortia influenced the AAU's emergence. Already twenty-four such associations and consortia of agricultural colleges, state universities, and Catholic colleges had appeared (Geiger, 1986, pp. v–vi; Gleason, 1995, pp. 44–46; Hawkins, 1992, pp. 10–13).

Yet the most significant precursor to the AAU regarding doctoral studies came from doctoral students themselves. In 1889, the Harvard Graduate Club encouraged similar groups to form at many universities. Within six years, the Federation of Graduate Clubs held annual meetings to maintain the integrity of the degree and to develop common approaches to graduate problems (Brumbaugh, 1939, cited in Semrow and others, 1992, p. 102, n. 185). At the 1896 Harvard meeting, students adopted Hopkins's doctoral standards as suitable for all doctoral programs (Haworth, 1996, p. 375). Such important decisions as this assumed greater significance as the federation's annual graduate student handbooks encouraged greater uniformity of practices among graduate schools across the country.

At the federation's December 1898 meeting, student representatives addressed two crucial problems that they then forwarded to the governing boards of major universities. First, they wanted standard policies governing residency requirements and the ability of students to migrate (that is, transfer) easily among different U.S. and European institutions—the Carnegie unit standardizing credits would not be introduced until the next decade. Second, they sought "uniformity in requirements for the doctor's degree" (White, 1899, p. 23). Significantly, many presidents and graduate faculty representatives of doctoral-granting universities also attended this meeting. President Eliot opened this event and also spoke of the migration problem. President Hall of Clark, President Butler of Columbia, and President Thomas of Bryn Mawr as well as faculty from Pennsylvania, Stanford, Cornell, Chicago, and California then offered their opinions on this and other problems. Professor John E. Matzke of Stanford praised the federation's efforts "in raising the standard of graduate work in America. Your *Handbook* has done much to set the different universities thinking, and I think it will tend to equalize the standard of requirements for the doctor's degree" (Bradley, 1899, p. 10).

Such institutional thinking had a more formal outlet when in January 1900 the presidents of Harvard and Columbia, along with those of Hopkins and California, invited fourteen other universities and their presidents to form the AAU. At their first meeting in late February at the University of Chicago, the presidents first discussed the student migration problem. They also invited a student representative from the federation—which they did for the next three meetings—to speak to them about the topic. Graduate students were thus a pivotal force in encouraging university presidents to set standard policies for doctoral education.

In 1915, the faculty formed the American Association of University Professors to represent their side of such issues. At the world's fair in California later that year, the AAU and the AAUP convened; they discussed recommendations on the future of doctoral education that emerged after graduate deans met there earlier (Hawkins, 1992, pp. 15, 73–75). Clearly, students, faculty, and administrators were creating formal and informal organizational mechanisms to guide the development of the doctorate.

During the next forty years, the AAU limited the number of universities accredited to offer the doctorate, publicly attacked nonmember institutions that did so, and determined the standards for their awards. Often, AAU's members explored the role and nature of the dissertation (see Chapter Seven for an analysis of an AAU discussion of this topic in 1902). Another function of the association was to inquire periodically about its members' doctoral policies.

In 1916, the AAU held its meeting at Clark University. President Hall reported on a recent association-sponsored presidential survey on university research. He reported various concerns about doctoral education in this first comprehensive assessment. Major issues included (1) doubts about the originality and meaningfulness of the thesis, as well as the process of choosing the topic; (2) ways to encourage student research skills and abilities; (3) assistance to new faculty in advising doctoral students; (4) the way new faculty members were overloaded with work; (5) ways in which the demands of World War I were forcing more utilitarian research; and (6) the inability to differentiate clearly between applied and pure research. Overall, Hall believed that universities were being asked "to become the center of intellectual life for the next generation" and must have the necessary academic freedom to pursue "truth for its own sake" (1916, pp. 105, 110–113).

Reassessments of Graduate Education. Ten critical studies on graduate education then followed as the Roaring Twenties and the Depression affected higher education (Berelson, 1960, pp. 31–32). In 1939, the Carnegie Foundation for the Advancement of Teaching published a study on early graduate education, as a means to rediscover the founding rationales for research and the doctorate. It examined the accomplishments of Hopkins, Clark, and Chicago. The study stressed that these institutions' successes, as opposed to those of more traditional universities, were tied to their meeting society's needs and offering their students intensive learning opportunities. The three universities had made "men rather than buildings" their primary considerations (Ryan, 1939, p. 141).

It was a subtle critique of the current national state of graduate education. The report signaled a need for change. Most graduate programs were now huge, enrolling some eighty thousand students across the country (Ryan, 1939, p. v). This condition stood in stark contrast to those programs that began at research universities. In this respect, the AAU held its member institutions to various elite quantitative standards related to the number of doctoral faculty, library development, amount of endowment, and so forth over the years. Although the AAU proved to be an effective vehicle for preserving the quality of the doctoral experience at member institutions, other universities and colleges demanded further expansion of accredited doctoral degrees. Many other universities offered doctoral degrees, even though they were not AAU accredited. Eventually, the AAU could not play the gatekeeper much longer, because students' and institutions' demands increased in midcentury.

Students' Reactions to Doctoral Study. Standardization pushed institutions to demand more exacting work from students. Many student reminiscences from this period focus on the trials of oral examinations. Virginia Gildersleeve, who graduated from Columbia in 1908 with a doctorate in English, reported that the final oral examination "included an immense number of detailed questions about the history of English literature" and that "no sensible person would ever try to remember such things" (1954, p. 55). Similarly, Arthur Schlesinger studied for his Ph.D. in history at Columbia from 1910 to 1912. In a letter to his fiancée about his comprehensive exam, he relates: "I'm so sick of cramming my head with facts and theories and views. . . . This kind of mental training I am now going through is deadening" (1963, p. 44). Probably, many students identified with Eleanor Dulles who studied economics at Harvard/Radcliffe from 1922 to 1926. She described the oral exams as "one of the hardest ordeals I had faced. I felt the strain but I did not fall out of the low window in a dead faint as did Harold, one of the male candidates. Nor did I rush from the room in a panic as several other students did" (1980, p. 95). She described herself as "in a trance from fatigue" after the experience (p. 101).

The dissertation received higher reviews, because it demonstrated the culmination of the doctoral struggle. Samuel Rosenblatt, a student of Semitic languages at Columbia University, characterized his dissertation defense in 1927 as a "delightful experience" (1976, p. 85). Schlesinger noted, however, that the defense "presented no difficulty because in the nature of things I knew more about the subject than my questioners" (1963, p. 53). Charles Kindleberger (1991) reported success in his dissertation, even though its thesis dissented from his adviser's economic theory. Others had rather negative reactions. Carroll Atkinson, an early critic of the doctoral degree process, had the darkest view of the dissertation: "The greatest disillusionment of the Ph.D. is the dissertation. . . . [It] is so hemmed in with mossbacked traditions that original work is nigh impossible" (1939, pp. 49–50). Finis Engleman studied for a Ph.D. in education at Yale in 1932. He characterized dissertation research as causing "discomfort for most students and distress and frustration for some" (1971, p. 49).

Regional Accreditation of the Doctorate, 1938 to 1957. Doctoral programs expanded dramatically between 1938 and 1957. During these years, the AAU and regional accrediting associations, especially the North Central Association of Secondary Schools and Colleges (NCA), struggled to find the right mechanism for doctoral accreditation. The American Council on Education and regional associations stopped using quantitative accrediting standards for its member institutions during the latter part of the Depression. Pressure then mounted for the AAU to conform as well to more qualitative criteria, which were linked to institutional missions. In July 1938, the NCA developed formal standards for accrediting specific graduate programs within an institution. It did not consider institutionwide graduate accreditation, which remained an AAU prerogative. Yet almost a hundred institutions offered the doctorate in 1940. Unable to handle the infighting between member presidents and graduate deans over appropriate graduate policies, numerous affiliation requests, and increasing organizational complexity, the AAU acquiesced. It finally stopped accrediting doctoral programs in 1948, leaving it to the regional accrediting associations (Berelson, 1960, p. 27; Geiger, 1986, p. 19, n. 61; Semrow and others, 1992, pp. 79–80; Hawkins, 1992, pp. 93–94, 201–206, 212–214).

Such developments not only continued the two-tiered system of doctoral education but also led to more practitioner-oriented doctoral degrees. First, universities holding AAU membership—and the ninety-two institutions active through its new ten-year-old internal organization, the Association of Graduate Schools, by 1957—were perceived as granting superior degrees. AAU graduates also believed that their doctoral degrees carried additional scholarly weight when they sought professorial positions. A later commentator on graduate study put it clearly: "The institution where a person gets the doctorate has a determining effect on where he ends up. The higher the institutional level of the doctorate, the higher the subsequent post in academic life" (Berelson, 1960, pp. 3, 113). Moreover, with the loosening of accreditation, other doctoral degrees were developed. Many discussions in this period centered around clarifying the role of practitioner-oriented doctoral degrees. With the accreditation of these degrees through the regional association, their numbers grew, especially the doctor of education, doctor of business administration, and the doctor of social work. The professionalization of the doctorate brought about great consternation among academics during the 1950s. Yet "the prestige of the Ph.D. has preempted the field" (Berelson, 1960, pp. 80–92).

Federalism and Doctoral Education, 1958 to Present. After World War II, national defense priorities fueled the government's desire to support research and doctoral education. Federal research projects, grants, and financial aid provided extensive funding for doctoral education to expand. Several events created a dramatic shift in direct funding of doctoral education. The passage of the G.I. Bill in 1944 filled colleges and universities with students who would not have been able to afford higher education. Graduate work was then within reach for many. In 1946, "the formation of the postwar federal research economy" assisted universities in expanding their doctoral programs. The federal government created the Atomic Energy Commission, National Institute of Mental Health, and the Office of Naval Research; each sought sites to conduct pure and applied research. Two years later, the blocked passage of the National Science Foundation was overcome, which created one of the most significant agencies to promote scientific research (Geiger, 1993, pp. 18–19). In 1958, the National Defense Education Act surpassed these enactments, significantly changing the relationship between the government and universities. To counter

Russian threats to national security after its launch of Sputnik, federal invest-ment in higher education reached $1 billion, especially at universities that offered the doctorate. The money went toward research, financial aid, and buildings. With the Johnson administration came the omnibus Higher Educa-tion Act of 1965, which further boosted monies for research and graduate edu-cation. Although the Reagan administration decreased student financial aid from $23 billion in 1980 to some $19 billion in 1983, funding returned to $25 billion by 1993 (Gladieux, Hauptman, and Knapp, 1994, p. 137).

Exponential Expansion of the Doctorate. Doctoral production increased sub-stantially during this period of federal funding. In 1960, 10,000 doctorates were granted. By 1970, some 30,000 graduate students received Ph.D.'s. During the next decade and a half, doctoral production oscillated annually, with some 33,500 students completing their doctorates in 1988 (Bowen and Rudenstine, 1992, pp. 20–21). Yet time-to-completion for the doctorate expanded during this decade, as Roger Geiger has noted, especially in "the humanities and social sciences, where the average duration of graduate study was seven and one-half years beyond the bachelor's degree (compared with just over five in the natural sciences)." Yet many programs saw less than half of their students graduate in the natural sciences, and approximately three-quarters received doctorates in the humanities and social sciences (Geiger, 1993, pp. 224–226). The era of fed-eralism thus created extensive research universities and opportunities for doc-toral education, a condition that has not appreciably changed (Trow, 1993).

Students' Reactions to Doctoral Study. Often the natural sciences provide a contrast to other doctoral work. As a Berkeley student rather poignantly recalls, in the 1960s science doctoral candidates' perceptions of the examinations dif-fered, depending on their department. A chemistry student confided: "We don't sweat course work or exams or the German requirement. The only thing that matters to the faculty is what we produce in the lab. The students who are asked to leave are the ones who spend a year trying to do research and make no progress." At the same institution, students in the English program consid-ered the comprehensive and oral examinations to be major hurdles. Students were known to fail these exams, and many postponed taking them until two quarters later than their scheduled time. In contrast to earlier decades, these two examples reflected the growing employment pressures on recipients and faculty. In 1971, positions for chemists with Ph.D.'s were more plentiful than those for English doctorates. Students believed that the program requirements were being adjusted to meet market demands (Breneman, 1971, pp. 20–25).

Contemporary Reassessments of the Doctorate, 1960 to Present. Beginning with Hall's 1916 study of the doctorate, scholars of higher educa-tion have produced critical studies of the degree throughout the century. With the support of the Carnegie Corporation, the most important and compre-hensive assessment was Bernard Berelson's *Graduate Education in the United States* in 1960. It launched several critical studies in the next decade, such as that by Heiss in *Challenges to Graduate Schools* (1970), Mayhew in *Reform in Graduate Education* (1972), Storr in *The Beginning of the Future: A Historical*

Approach to Graduate Education in the Arts and Sciences (1973), and Frankena in *The Philosophy and Future of Graduate Education* (1978). This plethora of works challenged the quality and equality of graduate studies, especially the doctorate. Advancing this inquiry, the Carnegie Foundation asked Jaroslav Pelikan to assess the issue in 1983. His title, *Scholarship and Its Survival*, echoed many people's concerns, as institutional retrenchments and declines in the number of doctoral students since 1973 pointed to a need for a dramatic reassessment. If downsizing were to occur, which doctoral programs should be eliminated? Attempting to answer such a difficult question and others later resulted in two national studies by Conference Board of Associated Research Councils in 1982 and the National Research Council in 1995 that ranked the quality of doctoral programs.

Although there have been many studies on the doctorate in the past thirty-seven years, no consensus has emerged on what steps faculty and universities should take. Until a broader agreement occurs on particular reforms, the basic 141-year-old structure of the doctorate will stand.

Conclusion

The American doctorate owes its lineage to the German research ideal. Yet its purpose, structure, and process have become American through six developmental periods during the past century and a half, as federal and state governments, accreditation officials, policymakers, campus administrators, faculty, and students have sought this means to professionalize candidates for the academic vocation. Calls for change have been largely ineffectual in creating systemic reform. Perhaps faculty members, who are those most responsible for training professional academics, still find this arduous process the most suitable.

LESTER F. GOODCHILD is associate professor of education and coordinator of the Higher Education and Adult Studies Program in the College of Education at the University of Denver.

MARGARET M. MILLER is visiting assistant professor in the College of Education and has also taught in the Graduate School of Social Work and University College at the University of Denver.

Although a student embraces a research methodology throughout a doctoral program, understanding and choosing a research approach will influence the selection of research courses, membership on dissertation committees, and the form of the dissertation proposal.

Research Methodologies and the Doctoral Process

John W. Creswell, Gary A. Miller

By the time doctoral students in the social sciences and education reach the dissertation phase of their program, they have brought a methodological perspective to their research. This perspective—gained through socialization within a field of study, mentoring by advisers, or their own initiative—shapes the direction of their scholarly research. This perspective is called a *research methodology* (also a *belief system* [Guba and Lincoln, 1989], *paradigm perspective* [Sparkes, 1992], or *inquiry paradigm* [Guba and Lincoln, 1988]), and it provides a philosophical base or frame of reference for approaching research that complements a content area of inquiry.

In this chapter, we explore the methodologies that guide student research, and we advance their centrality to three aspects of the doctoral process: the selection of research courses, the affiliation with faculty and a chair (adviser) on a committee, and the doctoral dissertation proposal. Although research methodologies have been explicated elsewhere (for example, Burrell and Morgan, 1979; Guba and Lincoln, 1988), their potential impact on the doctoral process has not been assessed. In addition, although a small, growing literature exists about the doctoral dissertation and working with faculty from alternative disciplines on dissertation committees (for example, Krathwohl, 1987; Locke, Spirduso, and Silverman, 1987), this literature has not been related to research methodologies. An understanding of the relationship of methodologies and the doctoral process can enhance our understanding of the experiences of doctoral students and add to existing knowledge.

We begin by assessing four research methodologies: positivist, which is the traditional quantitative approach to social and educational research; qualitative, also known as the interpretive or constructionist approach; ideological, an umbrella term for action and social change research that includes feminist, critical theory, and postmodern approaches; and pragmatic, a term implying that the problem is central to the research methodology and that researchers combine qualitative and quantitative methods to address specific problems. Methodological typologies already exist about the first three approaches (for example, Creswell, Goodchild, and Turner, 1996; Cunningham and Fitzgerald, 1996; Guba and Lincoln, 1988; Sparkes, 1992); by introducing the pragmatic approach, we add to this body of work.

To discuss these four methodologies, we advance five central questions about knowledge in social and educational research, drawn from Cunningham and Fitzgerald (1996). What counts as or constitutes knowledge? Where is knowledge located? How do we attain knowledge? How do we describe or write about it? Finally, how do we study it? After briefly assessing responses to each of these questions for the four methodologies, we present a study to illustrate how research might be conducted within each methodology. To facilitate understanding these examples, we have selected studies that all address the study of faculty research productivity in the academy.

Following this discussion, we turn to the doctoral process, suggesting that a student's research methodology affects how he or she selects course work, identifies and affiliates with faculty and a chair, and designs a dissertation proposal or study.

Before beginning our discussion, we want to advance several parameters. First, we view the four methodologies as heuristics rather than as ironclad, mutually exclusive systems. We address each methodology separately, however, to enable readers to conceptualize diverse frames of reference for scholarly inquiry more easily. As a heuristic, no single approach will rigidly reflect the precise belief of a researcher. The methodologies do suggest a general orientation to inquiry, though, and they derive from perspectives that philosophers of education and science have proposed in recent years.

Second, a doctoral program involves many, varied processes. We discuss how a research methodology influences only three aspects of a Ph.D. program. Future analyses might explore additional topics, such as methodologies and student socialization, mentoring, collaboration, and choice of subject specialization.

Finally, we delimit the discussion to the research phase of a doctoral student's program. Because developing a scholarly study is part of every graduate program, we feel that this discussion can be generalized to all doctoral students.

Research Methodologies

Authors from diverse fields of study have advanced several methodologies (Burrell and Morgan, 1979; Cunningham and Fitzgerald, 1996; Guba and Lincoln, 1988, 1989, 1994; Sparkes, 1992). These represent only a few conceptualizations, but they represent possible approaches from diverse fields of study. One can group these methodologies into four types: positivist (quantitative), interpretive (qualitative), ideological, and pragmatic.

Positivist (Quantitative) Approaches. In Table 3.1, we show how people use the four methodologies to conceive of the five issues. The positivist approach, associated with quantitative approaches to research, goes by different names, such as functionalist and hypothetico-deductive. Methodologies have come out of certain historical periods. Our image of positivism depends on how far back in time we go. In this discussion of positivism, we find it most helpful to conceive of an applied twentieth-century practice of inquiry rather than the fine-grained versions found in philosophical discussions in earlier centuries (for example, Cunningham and Fitzgerald, 1996).

The positivist approach views knowledge as something external to the individual, not based on the meaning an individual assigns it. For example, a theory of group interaction that explains the group members' behavior exists "outside" the group. The positivists believe that this knowledge is objective; it does not depend on the perception of any one individual. Thus, knowledge is located outside any single individual and is something apart from them.

Researchers attain such knowledge by engaging in studies that employ this "outside" knowledge. They start deductively with a theory and attempt to test it. Because their theory operates "out there" somewhere, they are confident that it will apply broadly to many situations and not be specific to any single context. It may be a universal theory that can be generalized to many settings or a narrow, substantive theory with little generalizability.

Because knowledge is objective and external to individuals, researchers want to make sure that their individual biases do not unduly influence a test. They therefore use standard terms to describe knowledge and remove themselves from the study. Researchers are invisible, in the background, out of sight. Their written study uses an impersonal tone. They define terms precisely in the literature and do not mention themselves.

To study something using the positivist methodology, researchers may experiment with careful controls for bias, use a prior theoretical framework, and carefully delineate specific variables that can be operationally defined according to standards in the scholarly literature. They set tight strictures to manipulate variables as in an experiment, or they design a structured survey instrument that measures the variables to make inferences from a sample to a population. They believe that information from a sample can be "generalized" to the population of respondents in a survey.

As an example of a positivist methodology, examine Jungnickel's study ([1993] 1994) of workplace correlates and scholarly performance of pharmacy clinical faculty. Jungnickel conducted a survey of pharmacy faculty to determine whether correlates explained variance in faculty publications. By building a conceptual model based on existing studies of research performance, Jungnickel felt that he could establish knowledge of faculty research in a theoretical scheme external to any one individual. This scheme would use objective measures that typified all individuals.

Jungnickel attained knowledge by starting with this model, testing it deductively, and measuring it on a self-designed survey instrument.

Table 3.1. Alternative Research Methodologies and Epistemological Issues

Issue	Positivist or Quantitative	Interpretive or Qualitative	Ideological	Pragmatic or Mixed-Method
What counts as or constitutes knowledge?	External-realist	Internal-idealist	Either external-realist or internal-idealist	Either external-realist or internal-idealist
Where is knowledge located?	Objective-dualist	Subjective-interactive	Subjective-interactive	Objective or subjective
How is knowledge attained?	• More deductively • In a more decontextualized way	• More inductively • In a more contextualized way	• Either inductively or deductively • Either in a decontextualized or contextualized way • Collaboratively	• Either inductively or deductively • Either in a decontextualized or contextualized way
How does one describe or write about it?	• Standardized language • Impersonal stance	• Language from participants • Personal stance	• Language from participants • Personal stance	• Language that fits the method • Use conventions within the method
How does one study it?	• Experimental studies • Nonexperimental studies such as surveys, correlations, comparisons	• Qualitative approaches such as biographies, phenomenology, grounded theory, ethnography, case studies	For example: • Feminist perspectives • Cultural perspectives • Critical theory • Postmodern perspectives	• Mixed method studies that triangulate, expand, or lead to instrument development
What study illustrates the methodology?	Jungnickel (1990)	Creswell and Brown (1992)	Dickens (1993)	Creswell (1997)

Although he controlled for intervening, exogenous variables, he relied on general measures of the context rather than a detailed knowledge of each setting for each individual.

In the final written study, Jungnickel carefully defined his terms (specifically, he measured research productivity), started with a theory at the beginning, and attempted to verify it through data collection. He returned to the theory at the end to determine whether the theoretical model held.

Interpretive (Qualitative) Approaches. As Table 3.1 shows, doctoral students using interpretive or qualitative approaches to research answer the five issues differently from the positivists. These researchers place a substantial emphasis on how participants in a study make sense or meaning of a situation. This knowledge resides "inside" the individual as opposed to "out there" beyond the individual.

People attain this knowledge by sensing their world and giving meaning to these senses through socially constructed interactions and discussions. The qualitative researcher visits the "field" gathering information from interviews with individuals who can tell their stories. The researcher studies these individuals in their natural setting for prolonged periods in order to gain a sense of the context or setting for participant's remarks. The investigator does not gain knowledge by espousing a rigid theory but forms it inductively from views and experiences of participants in the research.

The researcher, in turn, writes a study that reflects personal views of the phenomenon being studied. Because the researcher has been in the "field" gathering data firsthand, the account is up close and personal and uses the first-person pronoun "I" or the collective pronoun "we." Not only is the researcher not absent from the narrative but he or she is also mentioned as having personal views and interpretations. Hence, qualitative research is called "interpretive" research that reports participants' views.

This methodology involves one of the many interpretive varieties of research. It might be a qualitative case study of a "bounded" system such as an event, process, or activity. It might explore participants' views about an incident that highlights "culture at work" or the ethnography of a culture-sharing group. The methodological approach might build a theory around a social science concept that explains what participants in a study are experiencing. These methodologists might use other approaches as well (for example, phenomenology, biography, discourse analysis), but all forms of study design work from the meaning of individual experiences, build inductively, routinely use the pronoun "I," and hold that individual, contextual knowledge counts.

In Creswell and Brown (1992), we used this interpretive methodology in our grounded theory study based on procedures by Strauss and Corbin, 1990, which addressed how department chairpersons enhance faculty members' scholarly productivity. As a grounded theory study, it represented one of the many variants of qualitative approaches to inquiry found in the literature (Creswell, 1997b). We believed that the study would add to the literature because no extant theory explained the chairperson's role of developing faculty as researchers.

To build this theory, we needed direct knowledge from chairpersons, so we interviewed thirty-three of them. Only individual chairs could accurately frame this knowledge. The way to study this topic was not to begin with an established theory in the literature but to slowly construct a theory through in-depth interviews with chairs. Because individuals can never clearly separate their experiences and meanings from the context in which they work, we asked chairs to provide specific illustrations of practices and to talk about their own departments where they assisted faculty. Thus we collected a detailed description of practices and perspectives about faculty at different stages of their careers.

The theory slowly emerged as we analyzed and coded data. The actual theoretical model appeared at the end of the study, lending credence to an emerging design. The use of quotations and the personal pronoun "we" in the discussion helped make the study personal. Thus, we constituted knowledge based on internal perspectives and meanings provided by specific individuals; obtained information inductively through informal interviews; established specific working contexts for practices; and wrote the study using participants' detailed, personal information.

Ideological Approaches. Students employing an ideological methodology might proceed differently. By *ideological methodology* we mean those approaches associated with postmodern thinking, critical approaches, and feminist perspectives. Other ideological perspectives might be found in cultural, neo-Marxist, or lifestyle perspectives (Bloland, 1995). What counts as or constitutes knowledge may be external to an individual, such as feminist theories, or might be internal to an individual based on how the person experiences and critiques the world, such as postmodern thinking. Perspectives with a strong theoretical orientation, such as critical theory (for example, Morrow and Brown, 1994) and feminist theory (for example, Stewart, 1994), operate with an external or realist perspective, whereas postmodern writers eschew external theoretical orientations (called metanarratives) and critique or deconstruct them. Thus, what counts as knowledge varies, depending on the ideological stance.

All ideological stances rely on knowledge that is located within and negotiated among individuals, however. One would address a feminist theory about the patriarchy, for example, by asking women to reflect on their experiences and to negotiate the meaning of this concept through interaction with other women (or men). The knowledge can be either external or internal, so researchers using an ideological methodology either build or use a theory to explain the issues of marginalized or endangered people in society. They ground their studies in specific contexts and they seek to bring about change. This change may be only to deconstruct a situation, or it may be more active, such as to enlighten or emancipate individuals. Because this research is close to people, a strong element of collaboration between the researcher and those being studied may occur. Participants in a study often shape the questions, help in the analysis, and participate in the rewards of the research.

In terms of writing, the author and collaborators may be very much present in the text as they relate their experiences. These types of studies occur in feminist research that examine gender issues for women or in critical research studies that explore historical problems of domination, alienation, and social struggles. Researchers also use an ideological approach when they have post-modern perspectives that challenge the modern view of society's progress, growth, and linear development and that advocate a sensitivity to people who are marginalized, oppressed, and denied a "voice." A key feature of all of these ideological studies is that they start with a "vision" or possibly a theory about issues that need to be addressed in our society and they encourage change and active redress of problems.

Dickens (1993) completed a feminist study of the collaboration among twenty-six women faculty associated with women's studies programs in two research universities. She studied the role collaboration plays in feminist women faculty's construction of their own scholarly identities. Each of these women had collaborated with another woman on a research project, scholarly paper or article, or project in the creative arts.

At the beginning of the study, Dickens asserted that scholarship is a reflection of the women and the men who construct it, causing her to comment that her study is "openly feminist" (p. 3). Further, the study reflected her concern for women, a desire to place women at the center of her inquiry, and to reflect her own experiences as a woman and a feminist. She was attracted to the topic of collaboration as a means of encouraging change and challenging the hierarchical power relationships that characterize academic work. She also wanted to provide a voice for women as an "underrepresented" (p. 5) group and to discuss ways in which women express concern for and connection to other women. She based her qualitative themes of women's identity on affiliation, rebellion and resistance, synergy, pragmatism, and confirmation and empowerment.

By choosing to study an underrepresented group, challenging the traditional views of scholarship, exploring collaborative work, and focusing on a power hierarchy in academic work, Dickens's study illustrated the ideological methodology of research.

Pragmatic Approaches. Increasingly, researchers are combining interpretive or qualitative approaches to research with positivist or quantitative approaches. These studies are called mixed-method, multimethod, or integrated approaches to research (Creswell, 1997a). They might also have an overlay of the author's ideological stance. What counts as knowledge in these studies is both an external "out there" perspective and an individual perspective. The researcher gives both credibility while attempting to form some understanding of knowledge based on objective and subjective stances. The researcher starts with a problem that needs to be solved and uses the tools available to understand it. In other words, the researcher views knowledge pragmatically as based on studying "problems" or "issues" by using a variety of research methodologies (Creswell, Goodchild, and Turner, 1996). This means that a philosophical stance such as the location of knowledge is secondary to the larger question of the problem that needs to be solved.

The attainment of knowledge might begin with a quantitative study that deductively tests a theory and then refines it through in-depth qualitative interviewing. Another study might start qualitatively and inductively by using specific case studies to identify salient variables and operating theories and then deductively test the emerging theory with a sample population. For example, a researcher might begin a study with a grounded theory interpretive approach to build or generate a theory and then deductively test it with a representative of a population. The writing style might be personal during the interpretive part and impersonal during the verification or deductive part. To ease reading, the researcher might use either the personal or impersonal style throughout the study. In the end, the researcher has developed a mixed-method study.

We did not find a mixed-method study about faculty scholarship, so we designed such a study, relying on a common model for a mixed-method study in the literature (for example, Creswell, 1994). In this model, we would first use an interpretive approach. In the beginning of this study, we would seek a better understanding of the creative act of writing a scholarly journal article. In the first study, we would examine how several "prolific" writers understand the process and engage in perhaps three interpretive case studies. We ask the three scholars to keep journals about their experiences so that we can find out how they each write articles from their own individual approaches within their own contexts. In each of the three case studies (called a collective case study [Stake, 1995]), we do not limit our data gathering to published journal articles. We also collect writing samples, visit with students, talk with any living mentors. We assemble material from diverse sources to explore the approach of each author. Because writing is so idiosyncratic, we do not look to theories to explain the process but generate themes from our database. In the end, we have three detailed case studies of the writing process.

Now we bring in the positivist approach. From the three case studies, we expand the data collection by identifying specific variables as outcomes of the writing experience. These may include amount of productivity, time spent writing, and time spent revising material. We also identify variables in the cases that are likely to influence these writing outcomes, such as prior success in publishing, early guidance from mentors, and role of spouses. In both the independent and dependent variables, we build on our case study findings because new variables, not identified in past literature, have surfaced from our in-depth cases.

We now have a model of variables that we can test broadly among a stratified random sample of authors. We select three hundred authors from universities that, according to the Carnegie classification, have recently revised their promotion and tenure policies to emphasize more scholarly faculty work. We send out a survey to test the model and through regression analyses, we develop adequate predictors of our three dependent measures of faculty scholarship.

In summary, we have generated a model and variables through an in-depth case study and then used a survey to test this model with a representative sample of a population. The mixed-method study could be called a sequential, qualitative-quantitative approach with equal weight being given to each methodology in the study. The study's overall intent was to elaborate the qualitative part with the quantitative part to understand the issue of faculty scholarship better.

Implications for the Doctoral Process

What are the implications of these four methodologies for the processes of a doctoral program? We next relate the four methodologies to issues that doctoral students commonly address, limiting our attention to three: the essential course work and research tools that students need in order to conduct their research; students' affiliation with faculty, especially faculty and the chair who serve on doctoral committees at the dissertation stage; and the basic characteristics of a dissertation proposal. As Table 3.2 reflects, we have associated elements of these three issues with the four methodologies.

Positivist Approaches. The course work for an individual using the traditional positivist methodology helps a student identify a theoretical perspective to use, the methods to employ in a study, and the technical assistance needed to store, analyze, and report quantitative data. Theoretical perspectives are found within disciplines in the social sciences. For candidates studying higher education, the discipline foundation for theory may be in organizational studies, sociology, psychology, economics, or political science. Students need to seek out those theoretical courses to build a conceptual foundation for their research.

Beyond this, students need a firm understanding of specific methods of data collection and analysis. Foundational courses on quantitative research designs such as experimental research, survey research, or single-subject research are highly recommended. Furthermore, a course on measurement that explores the issues and the specific design of instruments can assist students as they prepare for data collection.

On the technical side, a student would benefit from statistics courses that address descriptive statistics, nonparametric statistics, regressions and structural equation modeling, and analysis of variance. Course experiences that enable a student to apply these statistical tools can provide a bridge between statistics and their application. Although courses in using computers are becoming obsolete, students need to master the use of computer programs, such as SPSS or SAS for data analysis.

Using the positivist methodology means that the student needs to select a chair and members of the doctoral committee who are familiar with quantitative approaches to research. A chair with quantitative experience is essential. In addition, the student needs a statistician on the doctoral committee, typically someone from the field of educational statistics. Recognizing that alternative types of quantitative approaches exist, we further recommend that students have a member of the committee with experience in the specific quantitative approach being used, such as survey research or experimental research. Under ideal circumstances, this individual might have experience in

Table 3.2. Methodologies and Doctoral Issues

Doctoral Issue	Positivist or Quantitative	Interpretive or Qualitative	Ideological	Pragmatic or Mixed-Method
Essential course work and research tools	Quantitative methods; measurement; statistics; computer skills	Philosophy and science of knowledge; introduction to qualitative research; field study (e.g., observational/interviewing); writing skills	The ideological perspective (e.g., feminist theory and methods); either a qualitative or quantitative sequence; selected readings	Qualitative or quantitative sequence followed by mixed-method course or selected readings; field experience in conducting a study
Discipline representation of faculty and the chair	Experimental researchers; behavioral scientists; survey researchers	Anthropology; sociology; psychology; and fields conducting qualitative inquiry	Disciplines with individuals who have conducted ideological research (e.g., women's studies)	Both qualitative and quantitative researchers; faculty who have conducted mixed-method study (e.g., evaluation area)
Characteristics of proposal and dissertation	Traditional scientific study	Variable design; literary; presented within a type of qualitative inquiry	Advances an ideological stance at beginning; data collection—collaborative	Contains both qualitative and quantitative elements; includes rationale for mixing methods and the type of approach

instrument design and could provide valuable assistance in designing the data collection instrument for the study.

In planning the dissertation proposal, students should consider the types of issues of paramount concern to quantitative, positivist researchers. When faculty members view a positivist dissertation proposal, they typically bring the following issues to a committee: the clear specification of variables; the articulation of a theoretical perspective; the rigorous application of research methods; the examination of validity, reliability, and generalizability; the question of bias and error in the study; and the proper choice of statistical procedures. The contents of a quantitative dissertation proposal also reflect these issues. The format follows a standard procedure of introduction, review of the literature, methods, and appendixes. Examples detailing this format appear in Miller (1991) and Creswell (1994).

Interpretive Approaches. Because students are often trained in positivist perspectives, those using the interpretive approach should begin course work by studying epistemological and philosophical issues (for example, What is knowledge? How is it attained?) that set interpretive research apart from positivist research. Students gain this framework through a course in the philosophy of education or the philosophy of science. Beyond this foundation, students need an introduction to the "standard" approaches to qualitative research. As books such as Bogdan and Biklen (1992), Glesne and Peshkin (1992), and Maxwell (1996) reflect, these approaches address topics such as the central characteristics of qualitative research, the formation of research problems and questions, typical data collection and analysis procedures, strategies for writing a qualitative narrative, validity or verification approaches, and ethical issues.

Armed with this introduction to both qualitative research and the process of research design, students can now specialize in one of the many interpretive or qualitative approaches to research. For example, Creswell (1997b) has identified five popular traditions in the social sciences and education: biography (for example, Denzin, 1989), phenomenology (Moustakas, 1994), grounded theory (Strauss and Corbin, 1990), ethnography (Hammersley and Atkinson, 1995), and case study (Stake, 1995). One could name several others—as many as twenty-five specialties (Tesch, 1990). The chief characteristic of these approaches, which are called "traditions of inquiry" (Creswell, 1997b), is that they are based in discipline perspectives outside of education. To obtain a firm grounding in them, students need to take courses in discipline fields other than education, unless education faculty specialize as qualitative researchers in one of these traditions.

Students should experience one of these "traditions" firsthand. We recommend that students engage in a field-based project in which they conduct a mini-study both to learn the application of a "tradition of inquiry" and to experience issues likely to arise in the field during data collection. This field-based experience enables students to practice writing an entire qualitative narrative. They will also explore writing issues such as literary style (for example,

Should I use storytelling or literary tropes?); composing a study within the "tradition of inquiry" (for instance, What is the rhetorical structure of a qualitative case study?); authorial presence (for example, How much should the author be present and "up front" in the narrative?); the use of quotations (for example, Should I use short, medium, or long ones?); and writing for an audience (for example, How does a scholarly paper differ from a journalistic account?).

In forming a committee for a doctoral student who employs the interpretive approach, we recommend that the chair of the committee both understand and practice the interpretive form of scholarly research. In addition, the more committee members have interpretive experiences and understandings, the less students need to argue that this approach is legitimate or defend their choice of a qualitative study over a quantitative study. Furthermore, after selecting a "tradition of inquiry," students need to find faculty members to serve on their committees with a background in their tradition of choice. These individuals may come from a discipline other than education, perhaps a cultural anthropologist trained as an ethnographer or a sociologist experienced in grounded theory. If the committee includes a chair and faculty less familiar with interpretive approaches, we suggest that the student "educate" the committee about qualitative research. Such "education" might include reviewing with the committee the criteria for assessing the quality of a study (see, for example, Creswell, 1997a) or sharing an important qualitative study with the committee before the proposal meeting.

The qualitative proposal itself is open to multiple forms, reflecting the diversity in qualitative traditions of inquiry and interpretive researchers' unwillingness to embrace a single model. Ideally, the proposal should respond to issues of concerns to qualitative researchers. For example, Locke, Spirduso, and Silverman (1987) address the use of literature in a qualitative study, the demonstration of the account's validity (or accuracy), and ways to handle field issues (for example, disclosure and reciprocity). We recommend that students closely examine the sample qualitative dissertation proposal developed at Harvard and discussed in Maxwell (1996). Maxwell reviews the format for the dissertation proposal for a case study project, and Marshall and Rossman (1995) and Creswell (1994) discuss this format for qualitative studies in general.

Ideological Approaches. A student using an ideological perspective should take courses that mirror either the positivist or the interpretive approaches. However, the courses need to include the ideological perspective chosen, whether it is feminist, critical theory, postmodern, or some other perspective. In addition, students need to engage in a field research experience in which they view the nature of the ideological issues and examine the potential for change and advocacy. Having this firsthand experience in advocacy for social, economic, and political issues provides an understanding about whether the changes proposed in the study will have an impact.

Doctoral committees and the chair should be knowledgeable about and experienced in the ideological stance represented in the student's research. Faculty from women's studies, educators familiar with critical pedagogy, or literary specialists familiar with postmodern issues can provide needed expertise. The types of questions the chair and doctoral committee ask of students using this methodology relate to a rationale for the ideological stance, the student's grounding in the perspective, the student's experiences in collaborative research, and the likely impact such research will have.

No distinct guides are available for the dissertation proposal. Students are advised, however, to examine reported studies in the literature. Although the approach will reflect either a quantitative or a qualitative proposal, the student should make several adjustments. At the beginning of the study, the student should clearly convey the ideological stance. The research questions should reflect change and advocacy for the group or individuals being studied, and the student should state clear implications of the research's impact as a rationale for the study. Students might consult standard methodological texts that relate to their ideological area (for example, Reinharz, 1992; Stewart, 1994) or examine specific studies (for example, Willis, 1977, for critical theory).

Pragmatic Approaches. The challenge for doctoral students who engage in the pragmatic approach is that they must become proficient in both qualitative and quantitative research as well as understand the interface between the two. Thus the research curriculum of a student who uses the pragmatic approach should begin with the essentials of the quantitative curriculum, such as courses in methods, measurement, and statistics, and should include the essentials of qualitative research, such as the philosophical foundations, an introduction to qualitative studies, and a grounding in one or more of the "traditions of inquiry." Beyond this, students need to learn about mixed-method designs. Few courses exist on this topic in colleges of education or other fields of study. To compensate, students must apprentice with faculty who have engaged in mixed-method research, read key books available on the topic (for example, Brewer and Hunter, 1989; Creswell, 1994; Reichardt and Rallis, 1994), and examine reported journal article studies (see Creswell, 1994). In addition, the student should build some experiences into the program to provide field experience in conducting a small-scale, mixed-method study.

For those students who undertake a mixed-method study, the chair needs to be familiar with mixed-method research, and the committee might be composed of individuals with both qualitative and quantitative expertise. Students might select faculty in evaluation, because evaluation projects often use mixed-method studies. During dissertation discussions about a mixed-method study, faculty members will inquire into the purpose of engaging in a mixed-method study, the sequence of the study's quantitative and qualitative parts, the relative weight given to each part, the extent to which a single study can cover quantitative and qualitative approaches, and whether the study will exceed a doctoral student's time frame and resources (see Creswell, 1997a, for a detailed discussion of these topics).

No guides are available for writing the proposal for a mixed-method study, but one can examine published studies to see their format and can extrapolate from these studies. The proposal should state that the purpose is to conduct both qualitative and quantitative research, and the research questions should reflect both methodologies. It is also critical to advance the rationale for conducting a mixed-method study (see the rationale in Greene, Caracelli, and Graham, 1989), to present a visual model identifying the sequence and relative weight given to both qualitative and quantitative parts, and to detail the methods of data collection and analysis for both segments of the study. It is especially important to identify how the results will be integrated (or kept separate) in the research findings; this area of inquiry is gaining prominence in discussions of mixed-method studies.

Summary

We have identified only a few implications of research methodology for doctoral students. Although students select research methodologies throughout a program, they often choose one of four methodologies popular in the social sciences and education today: positivist, interpretive, ideological, and pragmatic. A student's selection of a methodology influences their choice of course work, membership of the faculty and chair on doctoral committees, and the form and structure of their dissertation proposal and dissertation.

In this chapter, we have sketched the broad terrain of the doctoral process and research methodology, highlighting key elements of how these two broad facets of graduate work intersect. In this sense, we have expanded discussions about research methodologies and mapped the intersection of research and the doctoral process. Future studies can continue this discussion and students should consider these issues carefully during their doctoral program.

John W. Creswell is professor of educational psychology and a research methodologist at the University of Nebraska-Lincoln.

Gary A. Miller is professor of education and vice provost for undergraduate education at Biola University.

Using three scales and personal situational responses, this survey described the different attitudes and impressions that graduates and nongraduates (ABDs) had toward the dissertation requirements in a college of education.

Students' Attitudes Toward the Responsibilities and Barriers in Doctoral Study

Raymond C. Kluever

A major concern of colleges of education is the estimated 50 percent attrition rate from doctoral programs (Bowen and Rudenstine, 1992; Cesari, 1990). In other fields, such as law and business, the completion rate exceeds 90 percent. This attrition severely affects university and college resources, and the outlook for improvements in the 1990s is not encouraging. In interviews, students who have not completed their degree cite financial problems, shifts of interest, demands of work and family, discontentment with advisers and program orientation, and personal concerns as reasons for terminating their program before completing the dissertation.

Universities invest considerable resources in doctoral preparation by holding small seminars, providing highly individualized advising, and supervising independent research. Certainly, attrition has implications for efficient use of university resources, as well as for the individual student. Information that will lead to advising and program reorientation to increase the proportion of doctoral candidates who graduate will be of great value to both the university and the students who aim to complete the doctoral degree.

The purpose of this study was to compare the scholarly and academic credentials of doctoral graduates in education with those of nongraduates (ABDs) who only have their dissertations to complete. This study analyzed patterns in university programs and in student-university relationships that facilitate or impede degree completion. This study's results could cause universities to modify their admission standards, their guidelines for counseling and advising admitted students, and their efforts to retain admitted students.

Method

Participants in this study came from the University of Denver's College of Education. This college primarily enrolls doctoral students, along with a smaller number of M.A. candidates and certificate students. The sample included all 154 doctoral graduates between 1988 and 1993, as well as 111 of the students who completed all their course work and passed their doctoral comprehensive exams but did not complete their dissertations.

A survey form based on the responses from two focus groups and other appropriate scales derived from the literature was prepared and sent to all 154 graduates and 111 students in winter 1994. The survey consisted of three scales, along with questions about each subject's experiences with dissertation preparation, strategies they employed during the process, and attitudes about events that the students associated with working on a dissertation. Background information included items associated with employment while doing the dissertation, previous experience with research, local and distant places of residence from the campus, financial support, and ratings of perceived support systems. Subjects did not respond to all of the items. For this reason, there are differences in the total sample sizes reported.

Subjects completed three scales. These included a Procrastination Scale concerning attitudes toward dissertation completion, a Help-Hindrance Scale with ratings of helpful and unhelpful activities and events, and a Responsibility Scale that listed items rated as being primarily student or primarily university responsibilities. Results of the Help-Hindrance Scale and the Responsibility Scale are reported below, but the Procrastination Scale results are reported in Chapter Five.

The Help-Hindrance Scale consisted of forty-five items with eight choices ranging from "major hindrance" (1) to "major help" (7) and "not applicable" (8). The midpoint between major hindrance and major help was a 4. The mean scores for choices 1 through 7 were computed for each group.

The Responsibility Scale is a list of sixteen tasks that one must complete before receiving a doctoral degree. Respondents considered the sixteen items twice; first, they represented the task as presently practiced (as is), and second, they represented the task as they would prefer it to be (should be). They rated Responsibility on a seven-point continuum from student Responsibility (1) to university Responsibility (7). Mean scores of ratings were computed for each of the sixteen "as is" items and the sixteen "should be" items.

Surveys were distributed by mail to each graduate and student, with a stamped, addressed return envelope enclosed. The surveys for each of the two groups contained the same inventories and statements except for verb tense relating to completed dissertations versus dissertations still being completed.

Ideally, this survey would have prompted objective responses and personal impressions. In order to encourage this, both groups were guaranteed that individual survey responses would not be available for any faculty member to review. Identification numbers instead of names were recorded on each survey form. All forms were returned to a departmental secretary, who recorded the respondent's identification number and then forwarded the form to a retired faculty member for data entry and analysis. The secretary sent a second and third follow-up form to those who did not return their forms within three weeks. The secretary's records of names and identification numbers provided the names of those who were to receive the follow-up forms. Three weeks after the third mailing, no more completed forms were received and data analysis began. Completed surveys came from 92 percent of the graduates (142 out of 154) and 87 percent of the students (97 out of 111).

Results

Females made up 69 percent of the graduate group and 75 percent of the student group. Males made up 31 percent of the graduate group and 25 percent of the student group. The mean grade point average was 3.8 for graduates and 3.9 for students, and the mean GRE verbal scores were 529 for graduates and 546 for students. The mean GRE quantitative score was 494 for graduates and 533 for students.

The college allows students to specialize in ten different areas of education. Within each concentration area, the nature of the students and the expectations vary, which may influence how many graduates and students choose each concentration area. Students in off-campus programs on curriculum leadership and school administration have less access to faculty and university facilities and often find it more difficult to complete a dissertation.

Of the ten concentration areas, seven had percentages of graduates and students that were reasonable approximations of the proportions to the total sample percentages. That is, out of the total sample of participants, 58 percent were graduates and 42 percent were students. The other three areas had deviant proportions (more than twice the percentage in one group compared with the other). Two areas, Curriculum Leadership and Gifted and Talented, had proportionally fewer graduates than students; Curriculum Leadership had sixteen graduates and thirty-four students (32 percent graduates and 68 percent students), and Gifted and Talented had two graduates and seven students (22 percent graduates and 78 percent students). One area, Counseling Psychology, had a greater proportion of graduates than students (there were twenty-nine graduates [71 percent] and twelve students [29 percent]).

In the College of Education, it is not unusual for students to continue their employment in a school district or other facility while pursuing their doctoral degree part-time. The percentage of graduates who had full-time, part-time, or no employment is very similar to that of students. In both groups, males reported more full-time employment and females reported a higher proportion of part-time work.

Both females and males in both groups ranked employment and savings as the primary means of financial support while the dissertation was in process (Table 4.1). The financial support of spouses and family members was also common, whereas loans were a minimal source of support. Graduates gave Graduate Research Assistantship (GRA) and Graduate Teaching Assistantship (GTA) assignments significantly higher rankings than students did, but GRAs and GTAs were a minimal source of support for both groups.

Experience with research can help students complete a dissertation. Male graduates (66 percent) tended to have somewhat more experience with data analysis than male students (48 percent). Both groups had similar experience in conducting research (60 percent) and in publishing research. Only a minority (16 percent of the students and 18 percent of the graduates) of both groups reported experience in publishing a scholarly document independently. An adviser or faculty director may have provided consultation, but it was the student's project.

When students have contact with their advisers and easy access to university resources, it facilitates dissertation completion. Responses from this survey (Table 4.2) indicated that proportionally more graduates than students lived in Denver while working on the dissertation. Male students lived away from Denver more often than female students. A similar pattern existed for graduates; a higher percentage of females than males had lived in Denver, not outside the city, while enrolled in the doctoral program. Family circumstances may have been a factor in each of these events.

Students and graduates rated the degree of emotional support they received from different individuals while working on the dissertation (Table 4.3). Both groups rated the adviser and family as providing the most support and the dissertation committee as providing less. For these three variables, the mean rating of students was significantly lower than the mean rating of graduates. Other students (peers) were also ranked as less supportive than most sources. Aside from that, there were no significant differences in ratings between the groups.

Help-Hindrance Scale

Most of the item means (41 out of 45) on the Help-Hindrance Scale clustered in the range of 3, 4, and 5, suggesting that many items presented minor hindrances, had neutral effects, or provided minor help (Table 4.4). Items rated as major hindrances (ratings of 1 and 2) involved concerns about time pressures and financial or family concerns. Only one of the items was rated as a major help (a mean above 6 or 7); graduates cited persistence as assisting them significantly.

There were significant differences in response choices between graduates and students for twenty-nine of the forty-five items. On all except one of the twenty-nine items, students rated items as hindrances compared with graduates' ratings of those same items.

In a discriminant analysis that predicted the individual's status as a student or graduate on Help-Hindrance item responses, 81 percent of the individuals were predicted to be members of their groups. Predictions were more

Table 4.1. Degree of Financial Support

Source of Support	Graduates				Students			
	Females		Males		Females		Males	
	Mean	Standard Deviation	Mean	Standard Deviation	Mean	Standard Deviation	Mean	Standard Deviation
Loans	2.0	1.6	1.9	1.5	1.6	1.2	1.9	1.6
GRA/GTA[a]	2.0	1.6	2.0	1.6	1.3	0.9	1.2	0.9
Grant	1.6	1.2	1.3	1.0	1.5	0.9	1.3	0.8
Employment	3.5	1.6	4.1	1.5	4.1	1.4	4.6	1.1
Savings	3.2	1.6	2.9	1.7	3.4	1.7	3.1	1.5
Spouse/Family	3.1	1.7	2.6	1.7	3.2	1.8	2.7	1.8
Other	2.6	1.8	1.6	1.4	3.0	1.9	2.6	1.9

*Scale 1=Low, 5=High

Table 4.2. Proximity to Denver Campus
While Working on Dissertation (N = 213)

| | Graduates | | Students | | |
	Females %	Males %	Females %	Males %	Total
In Denver	53 (67)	28 (58)	33 (55)	8 (30)	122
Mostly in Denver	8 (10)	7 (15)	3 (5)	2 (7)	20
Not in Denver	17 (22)	13 (27)	24 (40)	17 (63)	71
Total	78	48	60	27	

accurate for graduates (89 percent) than for students (67 percent). These findings suggest that there are identifiable differences between these two groups based on their responses to the Help-Hindrance items.

Responsibility Scale

Students and graduates responded to only four of the sixteen items on the Responsibility Scale with significant differences. With these four items, students identified tasks as university responsibilities more than graduates did. The four items involved progressing through the dissertation, selecting a dissertation topic, locating research subjects, and scheduling the pace and time line for completing the dissertation. In a discriminant analysis, 78 percent of the subjects were predicted to be members of their respective groups based on their response to items. Proportionally more graduates were correctly categorized (86 percent) than students (65 percent). Again, as with the Help-Hindrance Scale, identifiable differences between these two groups emerged.

Student Recommendations

Students and graduates ranked ten tasks that may facilitate dissertation completion. The mean ratings ranged from 2.8 to 4.4 on a scale of 1 to 5. Regularly scheduled meetings with an adviser, seminars on approaching the dissertation, and a thorough understanding of college and university dissertation guidelines were rated most highly, whereas requiring a dissertation proposal before comprehensive exams was rated as having the lowest significance. On nine of the ten items, students rated preference for the support options more highly than graduates did.

Discussion

Responses from the survey items and the three scales indicated that individuals in these two groups had different attitudes and impressions. Graduates' responses suggested that they had a greater sense of independence and personal

Table 4.3. Emotional Support Received While Working on Dissertation

| | Graduates | | | | Students | | | |
| | Females | | Males | | Females | | Males | |
Individual	Mean	Standard Deviation	Mean	Standard Deviation	Mean	Standard Deviation	Mean	Standard Deviation
Loan officer/Loans	2.0	1.6	1.9	1.5	1.6	1.2	1.9	1.6
Adviser	4.1	1.0	4.1	1.0	3.4	1.4	3.4	1.1
Committee	3.0	1.4	3.1	1.3	2.5	1.5	2.6	1.2
Students	2.8	1.3	3.0	1.3	3.1	1.4	2.9	1.3
Family	4.3	1.1	4.1	1.2	3.7	1.2	3.7	1.4
Friends	3.8	1.2	3.4	1.1	3.6	1.1	3.3	1.4
Other	3.8	1.6	3.9	1.7	3.8	1.2	3.3	1.6

Note: 1 = no support, 5 = ample support.

[a]$t = -4.19$, $p < .001$; $t = -2.52$, $p < .013$; $t = -3.01$, $p < .003$.

Table 4.4. Mean Values of Help-Hindrance Scale for Graduates and Students

Help-Hindrance Item	Graduates		Students	
	Mean	Standard Deviation	Mean	Standard Deviation
1. Financial need for support	3.8	1.4	2.4	1.4[a]
2. Loss of free time for friends	2.5	1.1	2.5	1.1
3. Proximity to the university	3.8	1.9	3.1	2.0[a]
4. Library hours	4.0	1.7	4.2	1.8
5. Scheduling adviser meetings	4.2	1.9	3.2	1.9[a]
6. Conflict with dissertation director	4.7	1.8	4.8	2.1
7. Dissertation director's perfectionism	4.8	1.6	4.7	1.9
8. My own perfectionism	4.2	1.7	3.6	1.7[a]
9. My lack of interest in the topic	5.3	1.9	4.7	1.9
10. Faculty's lack of interest	4.8	2.1	4.0	1.9[a]
11. Choosing dissertation topic	3.7	1.7	3.1	1.8
12. Narrowing dissertation topic	3.7	1.7	3.1	1.8[a]
13. Finding a suitable adviser	3.4	1.8	3.8	2.0[a]
14. Dissertation process lacks structure	3.6	1.5	2.9	1.4[a]
15. Time management difficulty	3.6	1.6	2.9	1.3[a]
16. Lack of prior research exposure	3.8	1.9	3.4	1.7
17. Lack of prior data analysis experience	3.4	1.8	3.0	1.7
18. Obstructive committee member	4.5	2.1	5.1	2.0[a]
19. Lack of director's support	5.0	2.1	4.4	2.1
20. Doing the literature preview	4.6	1.5	3.8	1.6
21. Collecting the data	4.2	1.9	3.9	1.8
22. Typing/word processing	4.0	1.6	4.0	1.5
23. Job-related pressures	2.7	1.8	1.9	1.4[a]
24. Setting aside time for dissertation	2.9	1.7	4.8	2.3
25. Setting aside space for dissertation	4.1	1.6	3.6	1.5[a]
26. Getting drafts from committee	4.4	1.7	4.8	2.3
27. Lack of constructive feedback	4.4	1.9	4.9	2.1
28. Delay in starting after comps	3.8	1.8	2.6	1.6[a]
29. Conflict with family role (head)	3.7	2.1	2.8	1.7[a]
30. Inability to plan ahead	4.5	1.8	3.9	1.4[a]
31. Isolation from other students	3.4	1.5	3.0	1.6[a]
32. Adviser's support and encouragement	5.7	1.8	4.7	2.0[a]
33. Adviser returns drafts promptly	5.6	1.7	5.4	2.1
34. Collegial relation with adviser	5.9	1.6	5.2	1.8[a]
35. Self-direction	5.8	1.4	4.6	1.8[a]
36. Support of family and friends	5.8	1.5	5.1	1.7[a]
37. Willingness to take academic risks	5.7	1.4	4.9	1.7[a]
38. Organizational skills	5.9	1.4	5.0	1.5[a]
39. Time pressures	3.8	1.9	2.5	1.7[a]
40. Approaching dissertation in sections	5.8	1.4	5.3	1.6[a]
41. Ability to live with ambiguity	5.0	1.7	4.3	1.9[a]
42. Adviser expects completed dissertation	5.8	1.5	5.7	1.7
43. Love of the dissertation topic	5.6	1.4	5.5	1.6
44. Persistence	6.3	1.1	5.7	1.5[a]
45. Sticking to a schedule	5.7	1.4	4.3	1.8[a]

[a] Difference significant at p<.05

responsibility than students did. In previous studies, Wright (1991) has suggested that self-motivation and the ability to work independently are essential for successful completion of the dissertation. Hobish (1978) feels that including measures of personality is important in examining attrition from doctoral study. The causes of these personality differences are unknown from this survey but may involve individual circumstances, experiences, personal attributes, and self-management skills.

More males than females in both groups reported full-time employment as their primary means of financial support. Although both groups rated GRA appointments as a minimal basis of support, students gave them much lower ratings than graduates did. On a continuum of "much support" to "little support," students may have been at the "little support" end when colleges allotted support money. Alternatively, students may have had greater financial needs than did graduates; each group's ratings reflect this disparity. Students may have had greater expenses for family support and daily maintenance than graduates. Students may also have had lower-paying jobs than graduates had.

The Help-Hindrance Scale showed that both groups had financial problems. It is clear from this survey that earning money while working on the dissertation is a concern. Financial needs may determine how much time students spend on dissertation versus the time they devote to daily survival. Abedi and Benkin (1987) computed a series of regression equations to predict the amount of time-to-completion of the dissertation. Among the many variables in the equation, financial concerns were identified as the best predictor of time required to complete the dissertation. In a comparison of graduates and nongraduates, Benkin ([1984] 1985) found the major difference between groups to be financial dilemmas, as well as relationships with departmental faculty. This study and previous ones have clearly indicated that students' financial statuses affect their decisions about how quickly they will complete their dissertations.

Employment is undoubtedly related to students' financial concerns. Although it provides needed income, it detracts from time spent on the dissertation. Huguley ([1988] 1989) found full-time employment to be one of the major deterrents to dissertation completion precisely for this reason. The lack of structure in the dissertation stage is also a problem for many students. Germeroth (1991) summarizes some of the major barriers to dissertation completion. These include time and job pressures, as well as perfectionism (p. 64). She recommends that doctoral candidates remain on campus until the dissertation is completed and that they stay very task-oriented. A helpful adviser and committee are also very desirable components of the process. Wright (1991) recommends that a student who has been offered employment before dissertation completion carefully examine the position's workload. Wright also notes that having an acceptable dissertation proposal before leaving campus is absolutely essential.

Research was reported to be a relatively new experience for many individuals. Both groups reported some experience with data analysis but very little with publication. Although both groups saw preparing a proposal prior to completion of the comprehensive exam as undesirable, research experience aligned with course work might be able to provide a foundation for this later dissertation work. Preparing a dissertation is very different from passing courses and exams. It involves a one-on-one student-adviser relationship and independent activity, as opposed to class assignments which are highly structured. Throughout the preparation of the dissertation, there are no class assignments and peer relationships are different. Advisers provide direction and support, but students carry out daily activities independently, at their own initiative, and according to their own time lines. Personal, financial, motivational, and other perceived needs may impede completion of the study.

The aforementioned difference in the proportions of graduates and students in the Curriculum Leadership, Gifted and Talented, and the Counseling Psychology programs may relate to the programs' locations and patterns of operation. The Curriculum Leadership program is conducted both on campus and at remote locations throughout the state. Students residing in remote locations find it harder to gain access to advisers and university resources. A brief five- or ten-minute consultation is more difficult. In contrast, the Counseling Psychology program is conducted only on campus and is intensely supervised. Although this study revealed variations in the program's location, the results of other studies suggest that mail and telephone contacts can provide adequate communication with the adviser and committee. Each program must be carefully tailored to meet students' needs.

Completing a dissertation is an intense activity. For both groups, the adviser and the student's spouse and family served as the major source of emotional support and were most heavily invested in the dissertation. Other students and the rest of the dissertation committee were rated as providing little support. Because work on the dissertation is highly individual and there were no college-organized groups of students working on their dissertations who met regularly before 1993, the process can be a lonely one. Students need great independence and a strong sense of direction, especially to cope with a lack of research experience. It was noted that graduates gave higher ratings to emotional support from all sources than did students. This may be a significant factor associated with dissertation completion.

The scales and checklists suggest that there are identifiable differences between graduates and nongraduates. Because the differences are not great, the implication is that with some modification of procedures, a greater proportion of students can graduate. The first and last chapters in this volume outline steps that programs and students can take to encourage completion.

RAYMOND C. KLUEVER is associate professor emeritus of educational psychology in the College of Education at the University of Denver.

Research suggests that personal characteristics (dependence and procrastination) limit the likelihood of dissertation completion.

Psychosocial Factors Affecting Dissertation Completion

Kathy E. Green

An estimated 30 to 50 percent of doctoral candidates in education and psychology fail to complete their dissertations (Sternberg, 1981). Failure at this point is expensive and painful for the student, discouraging for the faculty involved, and injurious to the institution's reputation. Hence, researchers have tried to identify variables related to delay or failure to complete a dissertation. These variables include situational, program-specific, cognitive, and affective or personality factors. The issue of whether the doctoral admission and evaluation process should include less tangible dimensions, such as attitude and personality factors, is under consideration. This chapter reviews the role that these less tangible variables (particularly procrastination and perfectionism) play in a dissertation's timely or delayed completion.

This chapter briefly reviews the factors that researchers have associated with dissertation completion or delay. It then reviews the effects of two of these factors, procrastination and perfectionism, in greater detail and explores them further via a study conducted with education doctoral students and graduates. The chapter concludes by discussing what role psychosocial factors should play in our thinking about helping students through their doctoral programs.

Psychosocial Factors Affecting Completion and Delay

Researchers have examined the relationship of a number of psychosocial variables to dissertation completion or delay with differing graduate student groups. Most of the work in this area has enlisted education or psychology students, though the samples have included students of music, business, and the sciences. Most of these studies were conducted as doctoral dissertations, employed survey or interview methods, and were designed ex post facto.

Variables that showed no significant relationship to outcome or delay included fear of success (Stern, 1985), alienation (Girves and Wemmerus, 1988), level of femininity, achievement via conformance (Hobish, 1978), psychosocial maturity (Weiss, 1987), and locus of control (Smith, 1985; Wagner, 1986). Sample sizes in these studies ranged from 93 to 948 and were therefore large enough to detect simple correlations. The lack of significant results suggests a lack of clarity in construct definitions (the way definitions are operationalized) or very small effects, if any.

Variables that significantly predicted failure to complete or delayed completion of the dissertation included a history of separation or loss in childhood, high dependency needs, inability to plan ahead (Stern, 1985), lower levels of masculinity (Hobish, 1978), lower levels of persistence (Weiss, 1987), perfectionism (Germeroth, 1991), and elements of procrastination such as low frustration tolerance, rebellion, self-denigration, insufficient reinforcement or lack of structure, and task aversion (Muszynski and Akamatsu, 1991). With the exception of childhood loss, these variables center broadly around dependence. The literature suggests that perfectionism and procrastination are related and that both may be viewed as expressions of control stemming from deficits in self-esteem. Dependence may be a precursor variable, because it leads to action or a lack of action based on perceptions of support and control.

Wentzel (1987) found that internal locus of control correlated positively with time-to-completion, whereas the subscales for "powerful others" and "chance" were related negatively to persistence (versus dropping out). These results differ from the nonsignificant relationships that Smith (1985) and Wagner (1986) found between those variables. Wentzel used a different locus of control measure than the other two researchers. She also enlisted education doctoral students rather than psychology students or the university-wide random sample Smith and Wagner studied. These differences may have been sufficient to produce discrepant results.

For women, role conflict has also been noted as a barrier to dissertation completion (Germeroth, 1991). Hobish (1978) suggests that the dissertation process may be a more complicated psychological experience for females than for males.

There has been little systematic research with personality variables to explain failure or lack of progress in dissertation completion. Determining the relationship of the "big five" personality factors to dissertation delay and investigating the impact of task-specific aspects of personality would yield a greater understanding of potential connections.

Procrastination and Perfectionism

Procrastination is defined as the tendency to put off doing something until a future date unnecessarily. Previous research suggests that from one-fourth to nearly all college students experience problems with procrastination (Ellis and Knaus, 1977; Solomon and Rothblum, 1984), that the problem worsens the longer students are in college (Hill, Hill, Chabot, and Barrall, 1978), and that procrastination has negative academic consequences (Rothblum, Solomon, and Murakami, 1986).

Procrastination has been investigated in several domains (academic, decisional, neurotic, compulsive, life routine procrastination [Milgram, Batori, and Mowrer, 1993]). Academic procrastination is of interest here. The results of Milgram, Batori, and Mowrer suggest that academic procrastination is domain-specific rather than task-specific; that is, a student will procrastinate in every aspect of an endeavor, not just with specific component tasks. Procrastinators have been found to be more test-anxious, depressed, pessimistic, and perfectionistic (Rothblum, Solomon, and Murakami, 1986; Frost, Marten, Lahart, and Rosenblate, 1990). As research has shown, they have less self-efficacy, less perceived control, less frustration tolerance, and lower self-esteem (McKean, 1990; Frost, Marten, Lahart, and Rosenblate, 1990). They also have a greater fear of failure (Burka and Yuen, 1983; Rothblum, Solomon, and Murakami, 1986). Low correlations have also been found between procrastination and impulsiveness, extraversion, neuroticism, conscientiousness, locus of control, and achievement motivation (Aitken, 1982; Johnson and Bloom, 1993; McCown, Petzel, and Rupert, 1987; McKean, 1990). Several studies have shown no relationship between procrastination and achievement or intelligence (for example, Taylor, 1979). These findings suggest that procrastination includes affective and cognitive components rather than merely representing a deficit in study skills.

Milgram, Batori, and Mowrer (1993) found that the reasons procrastinators are likely to cite for their behavior do not threaten their self-esteem or reflect personal failings directly. For example, they endorsed time management more frequently than lack of academic ability as a reason for delay. Procrastination has been suggested to reflect passive-aggressive tendencies; the student uses failure to take action as a strategy to punish the person or organization making demands. If seen as a decrease or withdrawal of effort, procrastination has also been seen as a strategy used to maximize one's sense of self-worth; by reducing efforts, procrastinators can attribute failure to lack of effort rather than incompetence and can attribute success to unusually high ability. When maintaining a sense of self-worth is paramount, motivation to complete a task and anxiety about delayed performance become secondary concerns. Garcia and others (1995) found that the effects of procrastination were more marked in tasks perceived as being more competitive, ability-focused, and difficult. Certainly, writing a dissertation is ability-focused and is generally perceived as difficult.

Studies of procrastination have largely been conducted with community college students and university undergraduates. Most measures of procrastination address tasks central to course completion, such as term papers and examinations. An exception is the Procrastination Inventory that Muszynski and Akamatsu (1991) developed for use with clinical psychology doctoral students who delayed completion of their dissertations. Muszynski and Akamatsu found inventory subscales to differentiate delayers and noncompleters from completers significantly.

Perfectionism has also been noted as a barrier to project completion, because it is often used as an explanation for procrastination. Burka and Yuen (1983) suggest, for example, that procrastinators place unrealistic demands on themselves. Flett, Blankstein, Hewitt, and Koledin (1992) found socially prescribed perfectionism (parents' and others' expectations) to be related to the fear of failure component of procrastination. Frost, Marten, Lahart, and Rosenblate (1990) and Flett, Blankstein, Hewitt, and Koledin (1992) concurred that high parental expectations and criticism relate to increased procrastination. Individuals higher in perfectionism tend to have higher levels of stress and achievement motivation; are more neurotic, avoidant, dependent, and depressed; and procrastinate more (Fresques, 1991; Saddler and Sacks, 1993).

The purpose of the empirical portion of this study was to compare dissertation completers and noncompleters (ABDs) on facets of procrastination, including perfectionism. Graduates were expected to have lower scores than ABDs on all facets of procrastination and perfectionism. Furthermore, both graduates and ABDs were expected to endorse nonthreatening, task-specific reasons for procrastination more than threatening reasons concerning personal ability.

Method. The participants and method for this study are described in detail in Chapter Four. The present chapter describes results found from administering a modified version of the Procrastination Inventory (Muszynski and Akamatsu, 1991). The Procrastination Inventory contains forty-three items sorted into eleven subscales. Each item is rated on a five-point scale on the basis of how relevant the item is or was for the person while working on the dissertation (1 = not at all true of me, 5 = definitely true of me). Scale scores and a total score are generated.

This measure was developed to assess emphases in programs that require students to develop skills as both scientists and practitioners. It was argued that students with applied interests may experience difficulties completing tasks requiring a scientific orientation. Items were adapted from the Procrastination Assessment Scale—Students (Solomon and Rothblum, 1984) and written to tap facets of procrastination unique to working on a dissertation.

This forty-three-item measure was modified for use with College of Education students by substituting "education students/graduates" for "clinical psychology students/graduates." Item wording was modified to use past tense for the graduate survey and present tense for the student survey. A panel of three faculty, including a survey researcher, reviewed the revised measure for appropriateness to a population of education students and graduates.

Results. Subscale reliabilities ranged from .34 to .78 and were predictably low for the three subscales with only two to four items (need for approval, difficulty making decisions, unable to receive help). The internal consistency for the low frustration tolerance subscale was also minimal (.34). The remaining seven subscales had acceptable reliability. The univariate distribution for each subscale was examined for normality. Nine subscale scores were distributed reasonably normally, and two (rebellion and fear of finishing graduate school) were positively skewed. The skewness was not severe enough to warrant a transformation of these subscales. Differences in subscale scores were assessed using a multivariate analysis of variance. This test assumes multivariate normality and homogeneity of dispersion matrixes. These assumptions were reasonably well met.

Scores on eight of eleven subscales were higher for ABDs than for graduates, with a significant multivariate difference and significant univariate differences ($p < .05$) for seven of eleven subscales, as well as for the total score (Table 5.1). The main effect of gender was not significant, nor did it interact with graduate or student status. Surprisingly, scores on perfectionism were lower for ABDs than for graduates, though the difference was not significant.

It was hypothesized that subjects would endorse reasons for procrastination that were not threatening to their self-esteem rather than less personally acceptable reasons. Items were categorized as least and most threatening to self-esteem in the following way. Six items that dealt with the nature of the task rather than with personal skills were categorized as least threatening and were therefore hypothesized as more likely to be strongly endorsed. Six items related to personal ability were categorized as more threatening. Two aggregate scores were created for each person (most threatening and least threatening). Differences between most and least threatening reasons were assessed separately for graduates and for ABDs with paired t tests.

Differences were significant for students (mean for most = 2.9, mean for least = 2.4, $t = 5.2$, $p < .001$), though not for graduates, but differences were not in the expected direction. Students endorsed the more threatening items at a higher level than less threatening items. In this sample, students blamed themselves more than they blamed the task or university structure for their procrastination.

Students were classified by length of time since they passed their comprehensive examinations (less than three years, four to five years, and more than five years). There were no significant differences among these groups in any procrastination subscale score.

Differences between graduates and ABDs confirmed expectations. Muszynski and Akamatsu (1991) found higher scores for dissertation delayers than for those who completed doctorates in clinical psychology on five out of six of the same subscales. They found no differences in perfectionism, congruent with the results found here. They also found no main or interactive effect of gender. Flett, Blankstein, Hewitt, and Koledin (1992) argue that the relationship between perfectionism and procrastination is more complex than previously believed and that relationships exist only among subcomponents of each of these two constructs.

In contrast to Milgram, Batori, and Mowrer's results (1993), this study showed that procrastinators were more likely to endorse personal reasons over task difficulties when explaining procrastination. The disparity may come from

Table 5.1. **Means and Standard Deviations of Procrastination Inventory Subscales for Graduates and ABDs**

Subscale	Graduates		ABDs		F	p
	Mean	Standard Deviation	Mean	Standard Deviation		
Low frustration tolerance	2.7	.6	2.9	.7	5.9	.016
Perfectionism	3.7	.7	3.5	.7	3.2	.074
Rebellion	1.5	.6	1.7	.6	13.0	.001
Difficulty making decisions	2.8	1.0	3.1	1.0	5.4	.022
Need for approval	2.9	.9	3.2	.9	3.6	.060
Unable to receive help	1.9	.8	2.4	.9	16.2	.001
Procrastination as a work style	2.3	.7	2.3	.7	.0	.892
Fear of finishing graduate school	1.4	.7	1.4	.6	.0	.987
Self-denigration	2.6	.8	3.0	.8	13.3	.001
Insufficient reinforcement or lack of structure	2.0	.8	2.8	.9	45.4	.001
Task aversiveness	2.3	.8	2.8	.8	18.1	.001
Total score	2.3	.4	2.6	.5	31.5	.001

Note. The rating scale used had 5 points (1 = not at all descriptive to 5 = definitely descriptive).

Wilks' Lambda for Graduate/Student Effect = .75, $p < .001$, Box's M = 77.8, $p > .25$.

the differing nature of the samples. Milgram, Batori, and Mowrer enlisted Israeli college preparatory students who were initially low achievers. The sample population in the present study consisted of older people who were high achievers.

Discussion

Procrastination is associated with negative academic consequences. Interventions for procrastination have included study skills counseling and the introduction of external structure and contingencies. Rothblum, Solomon, and Murakami (1986) argue that because of negative affective factors associated with procrastination, these interventions may not completely ameliorate the behavior. One result of the present study addresses that argument. Although structuring the task is critical, ABDs in this study reported more personal skill deficits than complaints about the tasks before them. As a student plans a doctoral program, it might be useful to the adviser to assess whether that person is avoidant because of the task, because of internal reasons, or both. A student could address skill deficits through an extended workshop on research and dissertation writing.

Procrastination stemming from self-esteem deficits and dependency needs may weaken project control. The extent to which a student controls a project has been positively associated with ease of project completion (Rennie and Brewer, 1987). One study has shown that undergraduates who paced themselves had more positive attitudes and higher scores than when an instructor imposed scheduling (Roberts, Fulton, and Semb, 1988). These results argue for integrating student-controlled and student-designed reinforcements or incentives into the dissertation process. Incentives could include formally passing a series of landmark events (such as completing the proposal, obtaining approval from the ethics review board, presenting the study plans at a faculty-student lunch, submitting a dissertation progress log periodically, and so forth), completing a required research seminar for ABDs, completing an approved dissertation proposal prior to leaving the university, or attending faculty-ABD student meetings. Hatley and Fiene (1995) report that ABD students are "pleading for more structure, opportunity, encouragement, and mentoring in their . . . professional lives" (p. 2).

Group sessions using cognitive restructuring, stress management, and time management have successfully ameliorated procrastination. Franek (1982) discusses time management, negative emotions, motivational strategies, adviser-student relationships, and writer's block in a four-session program. Students who remain ABD for more than a year, or some other determined length of time, could be encouraged to participate in such a program. If students who are likely to procrastinate could be identified early in their doctoral studies, they could be directed to such a program at the outset of their academic career or could at least be advised of the potential problems facing someone with their profile. Similarly, students who have high dependency needs, a lack of persistence, or an external locus of control could be directed to tailored interventions. "At risk" students would be identified and the student and adviser would be made aware of the student's needs.

The literature suggests that persistence, dependence, and possibly locus of control predict dissertation completion. To instill persistence and increase independence and personal control, students could be required to undertake a research experience, probably in small groups, that continues for one to two years. They would need persistence to complete the project. Students would be individually responsible for portions of the project and so would be accountable both to the group and to a faculty supervisor. The group structure and the one-on-one work with an adviser would generate a supportive environment. Upon reaching the dissertation phrase, students would be more comfortable with the research process and might have developed a support network and positive research habits.

In many ways, graduate school is an apprenticeship and socialization experience. Students need to be socialized to doing active research as much as they need to learn objective skills. In order to integrate skills learned in different classes and to grow psychologically, students should have experiences that promote a shift from an adviser's direction to collaboration, from dependence to independence.

Doctoral students' scores on the Procrastination Inventory or similar measures can give advisers some sense of the students' psychosocial status. The adviser can discuss the profile with the student, making the student conscious of any problematic areas and integrating any concerns into plans for the student's program. Students who seem likely to falter can benefit from research groups, stronger mentoring, and tailored seminars.

At present, it is not typically necessary or recommended that universities select students based on their likelihood of completion. If university resources were reduced, however, it might limit the number of student positions. An evaluation of the student's procrastination, persistence, and dependency needs might then be advisable. Researchers would need to study the Procrastination Inventory's predictive validity more before anyone used it in this manner. Further investigation of the relationship between dissertation delay and personality measures is warranted by the sparsity of work in this area.

KATHY E. GREEN is professor of educational psychology in the College of Education at the University of Denver.

Which factors promote or inhibit the completion of a doctoral dissertation by nontraditional-aged women?

Nontraditional-Aged Women and the Dissertation: A Case Study Approach

Kathryn S. Lenz

An adviser talking to his advisee said, "You're here to study life, you're here to find out who you are. That's what this [dissertation] is all about for you." If the process of writing a dissertation and finishing a doctoral program is about finding out who we are, it is an adult development process. Often, major developmental processes require support and caring. In this study, nontraditional-aged women working on their dissertations spoke again and again of wanting a network of support and nurturing throughout the doctoral process. University professors need to become more aware that support networks and nurturing advisers could make a difference in women's doctoral degree completion rates.

The purpose of the study was to determine the factors that promote or inhibit the completion of a doctoral dissertation by nontraditional-aged women. This chapter presents the conceptual framework of the case study methodology used for the research, describes the nontraditional-aged women who participated in the study, and summarizes the study's results and conclusions. The chapter also lists recommendations for all important players in the dissertation process.

Thousands of men and women enter doctoral programs every year. Many of those entering students never complete the Ph.D. program (Sternberg, 1981; *Digest of Education Statistics,* 1992). Failure to complete a doctoral program has a negative impact on individuals, their families, universities, and society.

Individuals who complete all the course work for a Ph.D. program and successfully pass the comprehensive examination are sometimes labeled *ABD* (Sternberg, 1981). Many ABDs are women (Hanson, 1992) and are nontraditional-aged women (*Digest of Education Statistics,* 1992). There is evidence to indicate that graduate education as a whole has an aging and ever shrinking professoriat that reflects a Ph.D. shortage as well as shifting demographics (Weil, 1988). Faculty hiring pools are diminishing, possibly because so many people do not complete doctorates (Skelly, 1990). The need for Ph.D.'s to fill the faculty positions of today and tomorrow represents a supply-and-demand problem that higher education seems unable to address. If ABDs can be helped to finish the degree, it could ameliorate some of the faculty crisis in higher education.

According to the *Digest of Education Statistics* (1992), the number of women over the age of thirty-five enrolled in institutions of higher education has more than tripled since 1970. If more women over thirty-five are enrolling in graduate programs, why are there not more women completing Ph.D.'s? With its myriad social, environmental, and political problems, society cannot afford to waste or lose possible contributions from able women. There are no statistics showing exactly how many ABDs are women; however, if these women could complete a doctoral degree, the credibility assigned to the Ph.D. degree might give them the social and political influence to generate change.

The personal tragedy for women who are unable to maximize their potential is unmeasured. ABDs spend a great deal of emotional energy apologizing, rationalizing, and soul-searching for months or even years after passing the comprehensive examination and still not producing a dissertation (Sternberg, 1981). How this affects self-esteem and personal productivity is unknown.

Another important reason to examine the ABD situation is that university faculty and administrators regret when Ph.D. students do not complete degrees. The number of noncompleters diminishes the attractiveness of the university's program to new students (Weil, 1988). Weil also notes that the ABD phenomenon affects the faculty negatively. The university and faculty spend considerable time, effort, and money on these students; when they do not finish a doctorate, the university and faculty do not achieve their mission (Madsen, 1992).

The purpose of this study was to examine factors that influence nontraditional-aged women's completion or noncompletion of a doctoral dissertation. The results should enlighten university faculty and doctoral candidates about factors that may promote or inhibit these women's completion of doctoral dissertations.

The Conceptual Framework

The conceptual framework for this study is based on the perfectionism phenomenon and the self-in-relation theory. The following section will explain what these terms mean and how they fit into an analysis of the nontraditional-aged Ph.D. and female ABDs.

It seems valid to ponder how the development of self might fit into the dissertation process for nontraditional-aged women. Is self-development pertinent to the ability to finish a dissertation?

Theories in the development of self (for example, Freud, Erikson, Daniel Levinson, and David McClelland) tend to view human development as a process of separation (Gilligan, 1982). Male theorists almost exclusively used research on male samples when they devised the theory of development based on separation. In 1974, Chodorow argued that females develop normally through a process revolving around relationships. This idea later became known as the self-in-relation theory. A central theme in the construction of the feminine self, as the self-in-relation theory illustrates, is that "women's sense of self becomes very much organized around being able to make and then to maintain affiliation and relationships" (Miller, 1976, p. 83). The self-in-relation theory therefore represents a shift of emphasis in human development, especially for women, from separation from others to relationships with others. According to the self-in-relation theory, women primarily experience and fully develop the self (for example, becoming creative, autonomous, and assertive) in the context of relationships (Surrey, 1991).

In this study, participants' relationships with others in their lives were examined with respect to the role those relationships played in the completion or noncompletion of the dissertation. The data might show how relationships influence a woman's development through the dissertation process.

Perfectionism was the second part of the conceptual framework for this study. "Perfectionism is consciously and unconsciously built into the very cultural, psychological, and religious foundations of our achievement-oriented upbringing" (Hendlin, 1992, p. 5). Frost, Marten, Lahart, and Rosenblate (1990) show that two characteristics of perfectionist behavior seem to dominate people's personalities: setting excessively high performance standards and being overly concerned with making mistakes. Could these factors affect the completion of the doctoral dissertation?

Perfectionism ties into the stereotypes associated with low achievement that women fight in academe and the work world. This stereotype especially troubles women who pursue careers in nontraditional areas. To try to offset the expectation that they will not achieve, many women become more perfectionistic. Striving for perfection means putting personal identities on the line, because perfectionists equate performance with self-worth (Barrow and Moore, 1983).

Germeroth (1991) notes that perfectionism affects the dissertation-writing process in two ways: first, the candidate decides not to begin until she knows that the product will be perfect; second, the candidate is paralyzed by criticism of her writing. In her study of 132 Ph.D.'s and Ed.D.'s, of which 55 were female, Germeroth (1991) writes that the women were significantly more likely to let their own perfectionism inhibit the completion of the dissertation than were the men.

Participants

Five ABDs and six Ph.D. completers, all majors in education or science and all women, volunteered to participate in the study (Lenz, 1994). Six participants were students at or graduates of a small, private university. Five women attended or graduated from a large, state-funded university. Students from a large university's science department were included to see if dissertation issues differed for science majors compared with education majors and to see whether the university's size affected the results.

The term *nontraditional-aged women* refers to women who are at least thirty-five years old. This would imply that they had stopped their educations at some time. Participants in this study were between the ages of thirty-eight and fifty-three. All but one of the participants were married or lived with a significant other. The married women had children ranging from preschoolers to young adults. Table 6.1 describes the participants.

Methodology

Semistructured interviews were conducted with all eleven women. The interviews had enough latitude that each individual could tell her story. Probes (questions that the interviewer asked to help the interviewee explore ideas and issues more completely) were used to encourage each participant to give information about her dissertation process. The Multidimensional Perfectionism Scale, which Frost, Marten, Lahart, and Rosenblate (1990) designed, was administered to each participant. These data were used to analyze information about perfectionism gleaned from the interviews.

Summary of Results

Wolcott (1990) addresses anxieties about the accuracy of analysis in a study. In that vein, it is possible that the forthcoming analysis is not quite right. Wolcott also notes, however, that the study's participants may not have gotten things right either. With these caveats articulated, this section will now present a summary of the study and opinions about the most important issues, as reflected in the data. Objectivity was not a criterion as much as rigorous subjectivity (Wolcott, 1990).

Completers and ABDs definitely perceived and therefore handled the dissertation process differently. All participants viewed the topic as critical to completing the dissertation. Even when "completers" experienced setbacks in their selecting dissertation topics, they forged ahead to choose a new topic or to adjust the original one. The ABDs reported frustrations with their topics and allowed those problems to block their progress.

Referring to candidates' selections of dissertation topics, a completer in the field of education said, "I think it's very important that they find something that they will be able to stick with or have a reason to stick with." Another education Ph.D. said, "I cared about my topic an awful lot and I think a big part of this whole thing is that you have to care about your topic." Those candidates in education who had not completed their dissertations seemed stuck when they chose a dissertation topic that was then rejected for some reason.

Science doctoral students tended to choose dissertation topics that could be funded through professors' grants. This restriction made science students less flexible in their choice of a dissertation topic. Nearly all science doctoral students spoke of the need to find topics that could be funded. Stephanie, who completed her Ph.D., was the exception. She did not choose a funded topic because of the pressures involved, but she later paid the economic price.

Table 6.1. Demographic Information About Study Participants

Name	Status	Major	Marital status	Children/Stepchildren	University	Age
Beverly	Ph.D.	Physiology	Married	2 children	Large, pb	48
Hanna	Ph.D.	Microbiology	Married	2 children	Large, pb	48
Stephanie	Ph.D.	Environ. heal.	Married	2 children	Large, pb	42
Emma	ABD	Environ. heal.	Married	4 children	Large, pb	50
Joan	ABD	Science ed.	Married	2 children	Large, pb	44
Felicia	Ph.D.	Sch. psych.	Married	3 children	Small, pv	42
Martha	Ph.D.	Sch. psych.	Married	Stepchildren	Small, pv	38
Ann	Ph.D.	Sch. psych.	Married	2 children	Small, pv	46
Ellen	ABD	Sch. psych.	Married	Stepchildren	Small, pv	42
Sally	ABD	Sch. admin.	Sign. other	None	Small, pv	43
Rachael	ABD	Ed. psych.	Unmarried	None	Small, pv	53

Note: Ph.D. = Completed doctorate; ABD = All But Dissertation; Environ. heal. = Environmental health; Science ed. = Science education; Sch. psych. = School psychologist; Sch. admin. = School administration; Ed. psych. = Educational psychology; Sign. other = Significant other; Large, pb = Large public university; Small, pv = Small private university.

An ABD science student named Emma said, "Well, in this day and age where the topic drives whether or not you get the money is vital. Because if you can't get the money to pay for the supplies you need and the travel and so on, most of the time you can't do a dissertation unless you have some source of funding; so the topic's just vital." Funding dictated the selection of not only the research topic but also the adviser, because grant money is connected with a person.

Emma chose an adviser who was connected with the funds for her dissertation topic; she would not have selected that adviser otherwise. As time marched on, she realized that the adviser was not helping her finish the dissertation. Further research might define this difference in dissertation selection more clearly.

Selecting a suitable adviser or persons who could cochair the work was very important for the completers and appeared to inhibit the ABDs. An education Ph.D. observed, "I chose my adviser because I really respect her and I know her really well personally." Another education completer said, "I think that's probably the weakest part of the whole program, choosing chairpeople; nobody ever talks about it." She felt fortunate to find cochairs that fulfilled her various needs during her dissertation. An education Ph.D. chose an adviser who was accessible, patient, and knowledgeable about the university system.

Science ABD Emma said, "From the beginning, the study was sabotaged by my adviser's insistence on making that follow-up interview. . . . I could never talk to her." Emma felt sabotaged by her adviser's insistence on changing the schedule and the format of the original study design. This additional work appeared to Emma like a block to completion of the research. One ABD in education was assigned an adviser. That relationship did not work for her. Then an adviser who had been very supportive of her work left the university, which proved to be very inhibiting to her dissertation process. When advisers left the university, it seemed to plague the ABDs in education. Asked to describe the ideal way to choose a dissertation adviser, one ABD in education said, "I see the best possible situation is to pick a chairperson while you're doing your course work and actually be formulating your dissertation while you're doing your course work."

An established adviser-advisee relationship seemed vital to the dissertation process for all students. The ABDs lost their adviser-advisee relationships in various ways and could not establish new ones at the university. The completers remarked on how important it was that an adviser was kind, caring, and well informed about the logistics of the dissertation process.

Family and peer support were important to the completion of a dissertation. All completers had networks of support. An education Ph.D. commented that her best support came from those who had been through the dissertation process or those currently involved in the process. She said of both groups, "They helped me to understand [that] writing the dissertation was not only a mental but an emotional process." She added, "Knowing that you need to rally all the support services you can" is important for finishing the degree. Martha, a Ph.D. completer, said that her supporters had helped her by allowing her to talk. She said, "They listened. . . . None of them said I don't want to hear it anymore." Two education ABDs said they felt they had good support from friends, but the financial aspects of dissertation work had blocked their completion.

As the participants told their dissertation stories, they became strikingly emotional. This was true of ABDs as well as Ph.D.'s, regardless of specialization or university setting. Several of the women said they felt vulnerable while writing their dissertations. "Let's face it, you're kind of vulnerable in this process," a Ph.D. education completer said. Another Ph.D. in education added, "I really do believe there is a lot of nurturing that needs to take place to help people through the process." Because of that vulnerability, somebody needs to care deeply for the student.

All the women experienced great stress and emotional involvement in their dissertation processes. Stephanie, a Ph.D. in environmental health, regretted how much time her dissertation had stolen from her family. Her children, ages three and seven, had suffered greatly during her dissertation process. She lamented, "There were pictures on the wall down in the basement of my husband and the guys doing things. Where was I? I was never around. Or if I was around at certain times, I was not a person you would want to live with, because every minute had to be useful for something. That's why it was painful."

Both education and science students said they needed emotional support throughout the dissertation process. They all needed, but some did not achieve, a supportive adviser-advisee relationship. Stephanie, a Ph.D. in science, underlined the importance of support as she formulated the ideal situation for a Ph.D. candidate: "Just make sure that the person really wants [to complete a dissertation] and has a supportive group around." Two science majors who had not completed their dissertations bemoaned the fact that their advisers were either not helpful or blatantly unsupportive.

Time and money were concerns for ABDs as well as completers. Those who received their degrees seemed to carve out time to devote to the dissertation, whereas ABDs claimed that they lacked time to work on their dissertations. Money was a concern for both Ph.D.'s and noncompleters. Martha (a completer) wanted the degree so badly, however, that she worked several jobs to achieve her dream.

Theories

Support appeared to be an important factor that enabled completers to finish their dissertations in both science and education. Support came from varied sources for the completers. The ABDs did not cultivate the support they needed. They lacked strong adviser-advisee relationships, nor had they created a viable network of academic support. In addition, ABDs sometimes received negative input from family and spouses or significant others.

Self-in-Relation Theory. The completers had support for their dissertation work, which enabled them to finish their degrees. I called this support *positive self-in-relation input.* Just as support proved very enabling for the completers, the absence of positive self-in-relation input was an inhibiting factor for ABDs. Some ABDs seemed to receive negative self-in-relation input, which also drew them away from their dissertation progress. Relationships remained important to all the participants; it was the positive or negative nature of the relationships in the context of the dissertation work that seemed to affect the completion.

This information suggests a strong connection to the self-in-relation theory. If women need relationships to develop a strong sense of self, and if the self is reconstructed during a dissertation process, then relationships appear to be vital to that growth process. The self-in-relation theory indicates that simply having close relationships is not enough for female development; those relationships must be supportive in order for the feminine self to grow.

Perfectionism. All of the participants exhibited perfectionistic traits. The traits, however, appeared enabling for the completers and inhibiting for the ABDs. This difference seemed to depend on whether the participants viewed the perfectionism as inhibiting or enabling.

The Multidimensional Perfectionism Scale results indicate that the completers actually tended to be somewhat more perfectionistic than the ABDs. The data suggest, however, that the completers were able to overcome the traits of perfectionism that tended to block progress on a dissertation. An education Ph.D. said, "I don't like making mistakes, . . . [but once] I finished that [dissertation process], it really freed me up. It really did set me free as far as taking risks." For this Ph.D. completer, the dissertation process appears to have enabled her to relax some of her perfectionism. Completers may have overcome the inhibiting factors of perfectionism because they tended to have more positive support.

Those candidates who were able to overcome procrastination, the fear of making a mistake, and the need to set unrealistically high standards for themselves were finally rewarded by finishing their dissertations. An education Ph.D. said, "Intellectually if I stop and think about it, I know that I've done . . . a pretty good job. . . . But emotionally there's always this part of me that feels it is never quite good enough."

Some interview data indicate that advisers also suffered from perfectionism. A science Ph.D. said, "My perfectionism with my adviser consisted of wanting to look perfect to him." This appears to be an inhibiting factor for some participants.

Comparisons of Participant Subsets and Students Enrolled in Large Versus Small Universities

One important difference between science and education candidates was that the availability of funding usually determined which dissertation topic science candidates would choose. The funding source often determined the adviser, as well. This was not the case for education candidates; they had a great deal of flexibility in their choice of dissertation topic and advisers. Education students often let a passion or personal interest steer them toward a dissertation topic.

In terms of the emotional or developmental aspects of writing a dissertation, no significant difference emerged between large and small university settings. Most women expressed deep regret that the dissertation process had taken them away from family and friends. Some said they needed to rebuild their friendship circles after completing their degrees.

Both science and education candidates needed support and nurturing throughout the dissertation process. Having the necessary network of support enabled women to finish the process; those who did not have the support network did not complete the dissertation. An ABD scientist said, "I did not realize . . . at the time that what I needed was the nurturing community of learners that I was with to help support this process."

Recommendations

During interviews, the women who participated in this study were asked, "In the best possible case, what would the people in a Ph.D. candidate's life, including the dissertation chairperson, do to help someone finish the dissertation?" Speaking with deep emotion about the dissertation process, the women gave concrete suggestions about how the university, advisers, family, and friends could make the candidates' dissertation experiences more fulfilling. After synthesizing participants' comments, the author has made the following recommendations.

Candidates. Recommendations to nontraditional-aged female candidates working on their doctoral dissertations cover a wide range of issues. Each of these candidates should do the following:

- Be aware early in the graduate school experience that the dissertation belongs to her. She should begin searching for topic ideas and for adviser assistance as soon as she enters a Ph.D. program.
- Be assertive in questioning faculty members' research interests so that she can select an adviser whose interests dovetail with her own.
- Become involved in a research project before beginning her own dissertation research.
- Be open to dissertation topics and keep an ongoing list of dissertation ideas as course work proceeds. (Education candidates made this suggestion; science majors felt more restricted in dissertation topic choice.)
- Understand her needs and make them known to advisers early in the dissertation process.
- Learn when to let go of perfectionistic traits.
- Ask for help during the dissertation process. A candidate might need people to help at home, read drafts, and assist with child care.

These recommendations should give doctoral candidates some concrete ideas about how to help themselves early in the doctoral process and throughout their dissertation work.

Family Members and Friends. Recommendations for family and friends center around supporting the candidate in any way she believes appropriate. Here are some suggestions for family members and friends of a Ph.D. candidate who is writing her dissertation:

- Offer empathy and tons of listening.
- Let her know your relationship is in balance now and will be after her dissertation is done.
- Give her a sabbatical from her job, if at all possible.
- Do not sabotage her dissertation work by urging her away from it through guilt or shame.

Faculty and Advisers. Faculty and dissertation advisers have a great deal of influence on doctoral candidates. As faculty and advisers help nontraditional-aged women finish their doctoral dissertations, they could do the following:

- Establish collegial relationships with the women early in their Ph.D. experiences. (Over brown-bag lunches, faculty and advisers could establish an easygoing rapport with students that might foster the strong relationship needed later for dissertation work.)
- Discuss with students any ongoing faculty research that may help them to select dissertation advisers.
- Establish a kind, caring, yet professional relationship with advisees.
- Make the dissertation experience as positive as possible. It should not be adversarial. The candidate should hear support and encouragement, not just criticism of her work.
- Return corrected dissertation drafts promptly.
- Help candidates deal positively with perfectionistic traits and move beyond the blocks the traits may create. This may mean taking the initiative in setting deadlines and scheduling meetings.
- Be an expert on the dissertation process at the university. Understand all the schedules and deadlines and know the personnel responsible for each part of the dissertation process.

University Administration. The university administration might help nontraditional-aged women finish their dissertations in the following ways:

- Work to create a community within the university or college that would support doctoral students.
- Provide formal support groups for interested Ph.D. students.
- Encourage graduate student–faculty research teams.

Many university faculty members and administrators are concerned about the large numbers of ABDs. The comments and advice offered by these non-tradional-aged women will most likely help others as they complete dissertations.

KATHRYN S. LENZ is gifted education coordinator in the Poudre School District in Ft. Collins, Colorado, and adjunct faculty member in the College of Education at the University of Denver.

*In the humanities and social sciences, the time to finish a
doctoral degree, and especially the dissertation-writing stage of
the doctoral degree, can be significantly influenced if students work
in a collaborative environment; are not left alone in their struggle
to progress with their dissertations; interact with advisers frequently;
are given information about academic publishing; and have a
financial support package that fits their particular program and
research structure.*

The Institution Cares: Berkeley's Efforts to Support Dissertation Writing in the Humanities and Social Sciences

Maresi Nerad, Debra Sands Miller

With the introduction of the doctoral degree into U.S. universities at the end of the last century, concerns about the structure of doctoral degree programs in general and the role and nature of the dissertation in particular periodically resurfaced in discussions of graduate education. At the third annual AAU conference, which was held in Chicago on February 25–27, 1902, Mr. Wilhelm Gardner Hale, professor of Latin at the University of Chicago, presented a paper entitled "The Doctor's Dissertation." In this paper, he discussed the scope and character of the dissertation required of Ph.D. candidates. Hale described the qualifying examination and the dissertation as the two essential components of doctoral study. Together, they were to prove that the doctoral candidate was "worthy of admission to the higher profession of teaching" (Hale, 1902, p. 16). At that time, the Ph.D.'s sole function was to prepare students to become university professors—"complete" professors, in Hale's words—so the doctoral candidate had to demonstrate that he or she possessed the proper intellectual equipment for this profession.

Hale depicted the professor as someone who "should be within his own field, a transmitter of the world's accumulated knowledge and understanding, and an adder thereto" (p. 16). In order to transmit this knowledge, the professor ought to be a "cultivated person, provided with a great deal of knowledge, and with the power of imparting it—in a word, a polished polymath, capable of teaching" (p. 16). The qualifying examination was to test the candidate's general familiarity with his or her field.

In order to add to knowledge, however, the complete professor must also be a discoverer. To this end, the dissertation was to demonstrate the candidate's "power of originating for himself." According to Hale, a Ph.D. candidate could demonstrate originality within the dissertation in three ways: (1) by discovery, that is "the announcement and proof of something not known before," (2) by adjudication, that is the "establishment of one of two or more conflicting views already held upon a matter of doubt," or (3) by disproof of an existing view, "held upon evidence which had appeared to be of weight" (p. 17). Hale placed these three possible approaches in a hierarchical order, ranking discovery at the top and disproof at the bottom, while admitting that sometimes "disproof in one field may perfectly well be of greater consequences than discovery in another" (p. 17). This hierarchical system for evaluating the dissertation still prevails in the expectations of many faculty and students.

Besides the three types of dissertation research, Hale declared that the subject matter of a successful dissertation must be of measurable importance and "be of such scope that it can be treated exhaustively" (p. 17). He acknowledged, however, that "in the nature of things, no standard of measure, no announcement of a definable minimum could be reached by any amount of discussion" (p. 17). Although he was vague about the importance of the content and the dimensions of the dissertation's scope, he provided a very precise description of its presentation: the dissertation had to be organic, clear, and not "unliterary."

More than ninety years later, the discussion Hale initiated in 1902 about the role and particularly the nature of the dissertation continues. Today's graduate deans, faculty, and students talk about why we require the dissertation and what it should encompass. In 1990, the Council of Graduate Schools undertook a yearlong study to pursue precisely these questions. The resulting publication, *The Role and Nature of the Doctoral Dissertation,* summarizes "information on current policies, practices, and points of view related to the research component of Ph.D. programs, and from that information distills recommendations and ideas for improving doctoral education" (Council of Graduate Schools, 1991, p. i).

A perusal of the publication confirms that the dissertation's purpose and characteristics have not changed substantially from what Hale outlined in 1902. According to the Council of Graduate Schools, the dissertation should (1) reveal the student's ability to analyze, interpret, and synthesize information; (2) demonstrate the student's knowledge of the literature relating to the project, or at least acknowledge prior scholarship on which the dissertation is built; (3) describe the methods and procedures used; (4) present results in a sequential and logical manner; and (5) display the student's ability to analyze the results fully and coherently (p. 3). Significant changes have occurred, however, in the research environment and in the length of time it takes students to complete the doctoral degree. Consequently, this raises once again questions about originality, the importance of the subject matter, the dissertation's scope, and the form of the dissertation. (Whether the form of the dissertation is a monograph, a series of articles, or a set of essays is determined by research expectations, accepted forms of publication in the discipline, and custom in the discipline and in the student's program.)

Just as the Council of Graduate Schools reexamined the dissertation's role and nature in the early 1990s, so did the Graduate Division at the University of California, Berkeley. When this division studied the increase in time-to-doctorate over the past twenty years, it also assessed those two aspects of the dissertation along with other factors. In this chapter, we present findings from that investigation and explain why the Graduate Division at Berkeley made special efforts to support humanities and social science students as they researched and wrote their dissertations. We describe the institutional strategies we implemented to support students during critical stages of their doctoral study.

Lengthened Time-to-Completion of the Doctoral Degree

In 1990, the Office of the President of the University of California commissioned a study of time-to-degree and factors affecting completion. Undertaken by the director of graduate research at UC Berkeley and made public in 1991, this study examined time-to-degree on all nine UC campuses. The goal was to determine whether the time students took to complete doctoral requirements had increased over the last twenty years and, if so, what factors had affected the trend.

In analyzing the Survey of Earned Doctorates (SED) data for three cohorts of UC doctoral recipients over a ten-year period, the study found that the median time-to-degree[1] had increased by 1.3 years; in 1968 it took 5.4 years to finish a doctorate; in 1988 it took 6.7 years. (Mean time was 6.7 years in 1968 and 7.7 years in 1988.) An analysis of the data by major fields of study demonstrated that the length of median time-to-degree was the greatest in the arts and humanities and the social sciences. In both disciplines, median time had increased by 1.8 years, from 7.4 years in 1968 to 9.2 years in 1988 in the arts and humanities, and from 6.1 years in 1968 to 7.9 years in 1988 in the social sciences. Mean time for the arts and humanities was 7.4 years in 1968 and 9.2 years in 1988; for the social sciences, mean time was 6.1 years in 1968 and 7.9 years in 1988 (Nerad, 1991, p. 80).

This study also analyzed doctoral completion rates for only UC Berkeley students (see Table 7.1).[2] These rates varied widely across major fields of study. Students in the humanities and social sciences had the lowest completion rates. When the data from the cohorts who entered between 1975 and 1977 were

---

1. Median time-to-degree is calculated from the time a student enters graduate school until doctoral completion. It includes the time students withdraw from doctoral study or are away for research purposes. Calculations exclude students who received their master's degree from an institution other than the doctorate-granting institution.

2. Of all the UC schools, in 1991, only the Berkeley campus had collected data that allowed such an analysis.

analyzed, the results showed that only 31 percent of the humanities students and 45 percent of the social science students had completed doctorates after eleven, twelve, and thirteen years (as of May 1988). In comparison, the completion rates for biological and physical science doctoral students were 69 percent and 67 percent, respectively (Nerad, 1991, p. 103).

These findings prompted further investigations to determine at what stage students were most likely to withdraw from doctoral study. The research revealed a clear pattern: the majority of students left during their first three years of graduate study (31 percent), generally before they advanced to candidacy, and a smaller number (11 percent) left after advancement to candidacy, between the fourth and twelfth years. Furthermore, when the attrition rates of the humanities and social science doctoral students were compared with those of students in the biological and physical sciences for these two periods, the attrition rates were higher for humanities and social science students after they advanced to candidacy than before (humanities, 21 percent; social sciences, 12 percent; biological sciences, 4 percent; physical sciences, 8 percent).

To understand why students in the humanities and social sciences take longer to complete the degree and have higher attrition rates, the study examined the impact of financial support patterns on time-to-degree. Again using SED data for students who received their doctorates between 1980 and 1988, the study found that students whose major financial support came from their own or a spouse's earnings took the longest average time to complete their degrees (11.0 years). Students who were supported primarily by loans completed the degree in an average of 9.4 years. Those supported primarily by teaching assistantships took 8.3 years. Students with fellowships completed degrees in an average of 7.9 years. Finally, those supported by research assistantships had the shortest mean time, 7.0 years (Nerad, 1991, p. 89).

The study also showed that a large proportion of humanities students and social science students depended on teaching assistantships (humanities, 45 percent; social sciences, 25 percent) and on their own earnings or other sources of funding (humanities, 38 percent; social sciences, 40 percent) as their primary sources of support. A smaller proportion supported themselves primarily with research assistantships (humanities, 2 percent; social sciences, 11 percent), the most expeditious way of financing a doctoral program (Nerad, 1991, p. 90). In comparison, 49 percent of students in the physical sciences and engineering primarily supported themselves with research assistantships. Only 14 percent of students in the physical sciences and 26 percent in engineering supported themselves through their own or other earnings (Nerad, 1991, p. 90). It became clear that support patterns in humanities and social science disciplines were among the reasons that resulted in a longer time-to-degree and higher attrition rates.

To analyze time-to-degree and completion rates further, we conducted qualitative research consisting mostly of individual, semistructured, in-depth interviews on the Berkeley campus. This research corroborated the earlier

Table 7.1. Doctoral Progression Status for the 1975–1977 Cohorts in 1988

Field	Attrition Rate Years 1–3[a]		Attrition Rate Years 4–12		Pending as of Nov. 1988		Degree Awarded as of May 1988		Total N[b]
	N	(percent)	N	(percent)	N	(percent)	N	(percent)	
Arts	27	(34)	13	(16)	8	(10)	32	(40)	80
Biological sciences	73	(26)	10	(4)	5	(2)	192	(69)	280
Engineering	234	(37)	46	(7)	13	(2)	346	(54)	639
Languages and literatures	145	(37)	89	(23)	46	(12)	115	(29)	395
Natural resources	38	(22)	20	(12)	8	(5)	104	(61)	170
Physical sciences	168	(23)	61	(8)	12	(2)	479	(67)	720
Professional schools[c]	173	(35)	72	(14)	33	(7)	219	(44)	497
Social sciences	200	(30)	82	(12)	80	(12)	301	(45)	663
Total students	1,058	(31)	393	(11)	205	(6)	1,778	(52)	3,444

[a] Could include students who left after obtaining only the master's degree.

[b] Number of students who entered the program between fall 1975 and spring 1978.

[c] Includes architecture, business administration, city and regional planning, education, librarianship, public health, public policy, and social welfare.

Source: Graduate Division, UC Berkeley, as of 11/1988, "scr\attri–3–12," Aug. 27, 1990, mn.

Note: In May 1988, we calculated the completion rates for all cohorts. This means for the 1975 entrance cohort, thirteen years had passed; for the 1976 cohort, twelve years had passed; and for the 1977 cohort, eleven years had passed.

findings. We found that a series of factors rather than a single factor contributed to the lengthening time-to-degree (Nerad and Cerny, 1993). Combining what we had learned from the qualitative and quantitative data collected during the study, we developed a nine-point model to determine what conditions in addition to financial ones contribute to long or short time-to-degree or to high or low attrition rates. These conditions are (1) research mode, (2) program structure, (3) definition of the dissertation, (4) departmental advising, (5) departmental environment, (6) availability of research money, (7) financial support, (8) campus facilities, and (9) the job market.

The focus group interviews we conducted with humanities and social science students illuminated particular field-specific obstacles that delayed the process of doctoral completion, or in the extreme, prevented the student from completing the degree. We learned that for several reasons, writing dissertations in the humanities and social sciences posed more challenges, which was a strong determinant of progress toward completion.

First, in the humanities and, to a lesser degree, in the social sciences, the model of the lone scholar working independently still prevails (Nerad and Cerny, 1993). Lacking the laboratory, a collaborative environment typically found in the biological and physical sciences, students in the humanities and social sciences usually face a solitary research and writing experience and have less frequent interaction with their adviser and peers.

Second, these students encounter greater difficulties than their counterparts in biological sciences, physical sciences, and engineering when they cease to be "course-taking" people engaged in reading books and articles and become "book-writing" people responsible for producing original written material based on research findings.

Third, humanities and social science students often encounter a lack of consensus about what constitutes an appropriate doctoral research project. Although most agree that the dissertation must be original, substantial, significant, and carried out independently, the interpretation of these terms differs from one discipline to the next and often from one faculty member to the next. This ambiguity often provokes students' anxieties and may contribute to longer time-to-degree for humanities and social science students. Ambiguity about the nature of the dissertation also exists. Must the dissertation be a magnum opus or simply a piece of research in which students demonstrate their mastery of the tools of independent research and produce a modest contribution to knowledge in their field? We found that students easily lost perspective when trapped between two interpretations and felt insecure about whether they had undertaken significant research, treated their results in a substantial way, and presented them organically and clearly.

Fourth, the advising relationship emerged as an important factor in the dissertation process and doctoral completion, because the ultimate decision about the dissertation's scope and character rests with the dissertation committee, particularly with the main dissertation adviser. How might a student work most productively and still satisfy the standards of the dissertation committee or the major adviser? When, what, and how much should a student show the dissertation committee? How could the student best present the material to ensure positive and productive feedback? Doctoral students had great concerns about these issues.

Development of Support Structures and Programs

In response to these research findings and to students' concerns, the Graduate Division at the University of California, Berkeley, decided to implement financial support structures. These would address the financial circumstances and patterns of support unique to humanities and social science students. We also established an intellectual support structure to help students at the dissertation-writing stage of the doctoral program break the isolation, establish intellectual communities, overcome their anxieties about the dissertation's scope and character, and make the transition from "book reading" to "book writing."

Financial Support Structures. Given that support patterns in the humanities and social sciences tended to result in longer time-to-degree and higher attrition rates, we recommended that departments in these disciplines implement a support package. Such a package would give students an efficient mix of support for each stage of the doctoral program. It would offer fellowships for the first year, teaching assistantships for years two and three, fellowships at the conceptualizing stage of the dissertation, and then, if available, research assistantships for one year and dissertation-writing fellowships for the final year. Having learned that students often have difficulty making the transition from taking courses to conceptualizing the thesis, we emphasized that humanities and social science departments provide fellowships for a summer or for six months so that students could conceptualize and concentrate on writing the dissertation prospectus full-time and would not need to spend time on work unrelated to the dissertation in order to earn a living during this period.

Finally, because a large proportion of humanities and social science students support themselves primarily through teaching assistantships or their own earnings or employment, they often have trouble devoting their full time and attention to dissertation writing. During focus group meetings and in individual interviews, students frequently expressed the desire to have one full year in which they could concentrate entirely on writing the dissertation. In response, the Graduate Division reallocated its discretionary funds in order to offer a number of Dean's Dissertation Fellowships, primarily to students in the humanities. This fellowship provides a stipend of $10,500, plus resident fees for one year.

Three-Day Topical Interdisciplinary Dissertation Workshops. As we have established, students often found the dissertation-writing process to be a lonely, isolating experience. Some lamented the lack of contact with faculty, the lack of intellectual community, or their difficulty in establishing intellectual contacts outside of their departments. Many expressed anxiety about the content of their dissertation: Is it substantial? Is it significant? Is it original?

Building on an earlier model developed for the Social Science Research Council, Dr. David Szanton, now executive director of international and area studies at Berkeley, collaborated with the Graduate Division to introduce a new form of interdisciplinary dissertation workshops to the Berkeley campus.[3] These three-day, off-campus workshops, aimed at creating intellectual communities around common themes, bring together three to four faculty and twelve students writing dissertations on closely related subjects but in different disciplines. Students might come from the social sciences, humanities, and professional schools. Workshop participants share their research, identify common themes, and offer mutual support and constructive critiques from the different disciplinary and intellectual perspectives represented. In the exchange, students gain new perspectives on the individual proposals and projects and establish a basis for continuing interchanges, perhaps even collaborative activities.

Workshop planners choose topics after identifying broad cross-disciplinary themes. Identification of common themes is possible because Berkeley's Graduate Division maintains a database of dissertation-in-progress titles. Since the database also contains the names of faculty dissertation committee members, it is possible to identify faculty interested in the selected topic and to solicit their participation.

Once the workshop topic has been formulated, flyers describing the forthcoming workshop and soliciting applications are mailed to relevant departments and to students who, according to information in the database, may be particularly interested in participating. To apply, students submit a curriculum vitae and a copy of their dissertation proposal, or if the research is well under way, a current account of the project no more than ten pages long. From the resulting applications, twelve students, plus a few alternates, are selected based on the intellectual connections among the topics and the potential for intellectual excitement. The aim is also to include roughly comparable numbers of men and women, as well as students with diverse backgrounds, intellectual perspectives, and levels of progress in research and writing.

Students receive letters saying that they have been selected to participate in the workshop and later obtain the full set of participants' proposals. They are then asked to prepare for the workshop by imagining themselves to be the editors of an edited volume, with the various proposals as the twelve chapters of the book. Each student is to write a short introduction that lays out the relationships among the "chapters." Participants may choose to focus on common threads, linkages, conflicts, a distinctive critique, levels of analysis, clusters of issues, perspectives, and theoretical or conceptual approaches. All of the "introductions" are then redistributed to participants before the workshop begins so that each student can discover how others have read and contextualized their work.

The workshops are held off campus to reduce distractions and to create an atmosphere conducive to intense discussion and group cohesion. The night of arrival, participants are reacquainted with the workshop schedule and for-

---

3. An earlier description of these workshops appeared in Szanton, 1994.

mat, and the following morning the work begins in earnest. The first day of the workshop is divided into twelve half-hour sessions in which each project is presented for discussion—but not by its own author. Instead, a student from a different discipline, informed the night before which project he or she will present, is asked to offer a sympathetic but critical five-minute review of the project's major concerns and to raise three or four questions to initiate discussion. During these initial half-hour discussions, the project's author is not allowed to speak. He or she must simply listen to how other students with closely related interests understand and interpret the project. This structure encourages students to refrain from immediately defending their work and helps them hear new perspectives and ideas with an open mind. During these initial discussions, faculty are encouraged to remain relatively quiet so that students can find their voice and begin to cohere as a community of peers and future colleagues.

On the second day, the workshop begins with twelve twenty-minute sessions. Each author has five to ten minutes to respond to the comments, issues, and critiques raised the previous day and to begin articulating the linkages to other projects that may have begun to emerge. These presentations help prepare students for their future as scholars when they may be called upon to defend their work in a noncombative and articulate manner. In addition, they become deeply engaged in each other's projects. Afterward, with input from faculty members, students identify common themes and key issues. These become the basis of that afternoon's and the next morning's thematic discussions of emergent issues, problems, and conceptualizations that cut across the twelve projects. The workshop ends with lunch the third day after a forty-minute session is devoted to a brief evaluation of the workshop itself, to requesting written evaluations, and to planning various means of continuing to meet and extend the discussions back on campus.

Invariably, the workshops have been exhilarating and productive for student participants and for the broader campus community. Students have written letters about the workshops' successes. One participant wrote, "The workshop was absolutely invaluable in helping to define the parameters of a do-able study. Feedback on my proposal pinpointed the areas that need further attention, both in terms of methodology and basic premise." Another said, "The workshop exceeded my expectations by being not only terrifically valuable in terms of my individual work but also by creating the personal fabric of an ongoing interdisciplinary community." Students reported that in addition to providing concrete assistance with the dissertation itself and engendering an interdisciplinary community, the workshop's interdisciplinary aspect clarified their commitments to their own disciplines and helped them articulate for themselves and for others the roots of their own intellectual assumptions and disciplinary identities. They forgot their fears of having chosen an unsubstantial, insignificant, or unoriginal topic.

Because hundreds of graduate students could benefit from the dissertation workshops or similar gatherings, and because we recognize that, alone, we can serve only a small fraction of the campus's graduate students, we are gratified that the dissertation workshops' success extends beyond just the individual students who participate. The pedagogy of the dissertation workshop is beginning to seep into seminars on campus as some of the faculty involved in the dissertation workshops have people present each other's work in their own classes. In addition, faculty members are beginning to organize dissertation workshops in their own departments or areas of interest in order to build a broader interdisciplinary community and to foster campuswide intellectual networks. Finally, the Graduate Division, International and Area Studies (IAS), and the University Library staff have collaborated to devise ways of having doctoral students identify topics and organize the actual workshops.

Dissertations-in-Progress Abstract. UC Berkeley has established a new database called "Abstracts of UC Berkeley Dissertations-in-Progress" (ADP) on a university library Web page that students can easily search. The university library technical staff designed and maintains the database, and the Graduate Division is responsible for collecting and entering the abstracts. In addition to the 250-to-300-word accounts of the dissertation (which the student can revise at any time), the abstracts also include information on how to contact the author. To encourage students to put abstracts in the database and to work with other students, the library has designated a set of seminar rooms in which groups of doctoral students can meet regularly. As further incentives, the Graduate Division is offering "coffee and donuts" funding to make the meetings more conducive to collegiality, and IAS has offered to provide both general advice on meeting formats and to explore with interested groups the possibilities of organizing and funding a Three-Day Topical Interdisciplinary Dissertation Workshop.

Practical Strategies for Writing a Dissertation. To address students' problems with the practical aspects of producing a substantial, significant, and original dissertation written in an "organic, clear, and not *un*literary" way, as Hale put it in 1902, the Graduate Division collaborated with an outside writing consultant. Dr. Dorothy Duff Brown, a UC Berkeley Ph.D., helped the Graduate Division develop the popular workshops on dissertation writing entitled "Practical Strategies for Writing a Dissertation." From individual interviews with students in the humanities and social sciences who took a long time to complete their dissertations and from our monthly focus group meetings with current students in those disciplines, we identified the practical considerations behind students' concerns about writing the dissertation: Where and how do we begin? What are some useful tips for planning and outlining? How do we make the transition from data collection, literature review, and field research to writing? Are there some basic time management skills for scholars? When should one show sections of the dissertation to one's adviser? How can one assist the adviser in giving practical comments? How does one sustain motivation and complete the dissertation?

In response to these questions, the Graduate Division offered the first "Practical Strategies" workshop in 1990. During the next year and a half, we continued to conduct focus groups after each workshop. Based on participants' reflections and comments, we refined the workshops until they achieved their current format.

Exactly as their title suggests, the dissertation workshops focus on the pragmatic aspects of writing the dissertation. Building on what we knew to be the major problems for students, we structured the workshops around coping with three basic areas: materials, time, and people. These workshops have proven successful in helping students organize their research and write the dissertation. The next few pages will describe them in greater length.

Materials. Producing a dissertation involves not only writing down ideas but also assembling a concrete, physical manuscript. Consequently, the workshop emphasizes utilizing the materials necessary to organize and generate a dissertation. To help writers avoid the pitfalls of abstract planning and to assist them in realizing the finished product, the workshop suggests that students work with concrete tools. Dissertation writers are advised to have a loose-leaf binder that represents the dissertation. Dividers should indicate all its sections and chapters and an appropriate number of blank pages should stand for each section or chapter. As a page of the dissertation is produced, it is inserted into the binder and the blank representational page is removed.

Planning and Outlining. Students are advised to generate a table of contents rather than an outline as the primary organizing tool for the dissertation. By developing a table of contents, the writer can see the whole as well as the parts. In addition, whereas an outline sends a subliminal message that the work is open-ended, can be changed, added to, or fixed, the table of contents stands as an index to a completed work, relating parts to a whole and implying a certain soundness. This, in turn, creates a sense of coherence in the writer's mind. Seeing a table of contents also prompts faculty to suggest changes within the defined structure, while respecting the integrity of the work presented.

One creative way to generate a table of contents is to draw a cognitive map. This map allows ideas to develop organically as a reflection of what the writer already knows about his or her topic. This intuitive, visual brainstorming, easily accomplished on a large sheet of paper, shows the relationships between thoughts or groups of ideas and often reveals the ideas' relative weight or importance. New connections between ideas emerge in the mapping process; sequences, parallels, subordinations, and complementarities all come to light. Maps are fast and easy to make. They are also fun, because they reflect the organic processes of the writer's mind and because it is not stressful to work on them. In addition, the map aids and permits creativity. Finally, the map is easily translated back into linear form, in this case, a table of contents.

Organizing Materials. Once writers have conceptualized the body of the dissertation, they should organize reference materials and notes according to their table of contents. Students are encouraged to think carefully about their filing system. One possible method is to organize dissertation notes in a simple cardboard file holder and a set of file folders with tabs. Each file folder is to be labeled provisionally, in pencil, according to the sections of the completed dissertation: abstract, prefatory material, table of contents, chapters, list of tables, illustrations, appendixes, and so forth. In addition, the file box will contain a folder for memos to the dissertation adviser and committee members. All notes that are germane to the text should go in the appropriate folder. This process requires that the writer make an initial decision about chapter content. Although the advice on materials may seem trivial, we found that students are grateful for the discussion of these practical organizational strategies that faculty rarely address.

Transition to Writing. Students can easily compile this assortment of materials and notes in the dissertation binder with removable tape. They can tape notes in any form to the pages in the loose-leaf notebook and assemble them in the shape of the manuscript. The process of pasting together a section of text gives the writer the freedom to make early, provisional decisions. After writing a chapter, the student can place the whole chapter in the binder. These physical decisions force the writer to avoid abstractions. With this system, it is also easier to make and keep track of changes in the course of composing. This process fosters a playfulness that stimulates and enhances creativity and that can break the most stultifying writer's block.

Time. The second segment of the workshop addresses the matter of time management. Unlike students in the sciences, who organize their research according to the schedule of the lab and whose dissertation-writing time is much shorter, students in the humanities and social sciences work alone and must learn to structure their own time. First, the workshop encourages students to establish a realistic daily work schedule and to try to be faithful to it. A good strategy for accomplishing this is to set the daily hour at which work on the dissertation will cease and to stop at that time. Achieving a firm control over the stopping time helps establish much better control over the starting time, because one is more likely to begin working early in order to accomplish what must be done for the day.

Second, the workshop stresses the importance of setting priorities for each work session. For example, a ten-minute planning session before the daily cut-off time may be sufficient for setting the next session's priorities and for producing momentum for the next day's work.

Third, it is important to recognize that having unlimited time does not guarantee greater productivity. Often, writers constrained by a more structured schedule, even limited work hours, are more productive and more likely to stay on track with the dissertation project than those with unlimited time at their disposal. Consequently, setting a target number of hours per week to work on the dissertation is recommended. The workshop emphasizes repeatedly that mental refreshment is essential to successful completion. A regular day off is necessary, regardless of whether the writer maintained the weekly schedule or not.

People. The third part of the workshop addresses the often delicate interaction with the dissertation adviser and committee members. To ensure that students receive good feedback on their dissertation, the workshop encourages students to think of themselves as the project manager who must fruit-fully manage relationships with committee members. One of the keys to this task is to use the memo effectually. With each submission of material to the adviser or committee members, the student should accompany the dissertation text with a memo stating exactly what is being submitted and where this piece fits into the dissertation in terms of the table of contents. Such a memo should also make comments about the major points or arguments presented in the writing and should detail what feedback is being requested. Finally, the memo should establish how the student will get back in touch with the faculty. Focusing on this aspect of the adviser-advisee relationship proves productive, because students tend to forget about the mundane aspects of this interaction or depend completely on the adviser's initiative in commenting on and returning material.

Outcomes. The five-hour "Practical Strategies for Writing a Dissertation" workshops continue to be one of the most popular programs that the Graduate Division offers in support of doctoral students. Each fall and spring semester, all doctoral students in humanities and social science departments who were advanced to candidacy the previous semester receive an invitational flyer informing them about the workshop and a return postcard to facilitate enrollment. Workshops are always full and there is inevitably a waiting list.

Another outcome of the workshop is that participants recognize that others have problems with the day-to-day mechanics of dissertation writing. They come to see that they do not have an intellectual deficiency that renders them unable to accomplish the task. These realizations help relieve guilt and propel participants toward the premise of the workshop—that there is a practical approach to dissertation writing that, in spite of students' anxieties and insecurities about the nature of the dissertation-writing process, will make the project doable.

Students often continue meeting with each other in pairs or in groups, applying the information and the models they have learned to the writing process. By repeatedly delivering sound information, the institution implicitly gives all doctoral students in the humanities and social sciences the message that using practical strategies can help them complete the dissertation and the doctoral degree.

Academic Publishing Workshop. Besides being a demonstration of originality and a test of the doctoral candidate's ability to undertake scholarly research, the dissertation is also a product. Only when it is published does this product become accessible to an audience other than the dissertation committee. The implicit (or explicit) expectation that a dissertation, or at least portions of it, should be published often makes the dissertation writer anxious, inhibits the writing in anticipation of publishing (particularly in fields in which the dissertation is regarded as the magnum opus), and may slow progress toward degree completion.

To ease students' anxieties about publishing and to clarify the process of academic publishing, the Graduate Division developed and presented

"Academic Publishing for Graduate Students in the Humanities and Social Sciences." This workshop was designed to address faculty's and departments' approaches and attitudes toward publishing and to provide students with information about publishing dissertations as journal articles or books through an academic press.

This two-hour workshop had a panel composed of faculty members in the humanities and social sciences, editors at the Stanford University Press and the University of California Press, student editors of campus publications, and two recent Berkeley Ph.D. recipients who had book contracts. These panel members answered the most commonly asked questions about publishing journal articles and the dissertation and presented their viewpoints and suggestions on whether, when, and how to publish.

In order to make this information available to all students, the Graduate Division produced *Academic Publishing: A Guide for UC Berkeley Graduate Students in the Humanities and Social Sciences,* which draws on the information presented in the publishing workshop. The first section of the guide discusses the merits, drawbacks, and process of publishing journal articles as a graduate student. The second section addresses what is involved in turning the dissertation into a book, considers the likelihood and process of publishing the dissertation as a book and the publishers' perspective on dissertation publishing, and examines a variety of publishing options. The final section includes recommended references, sample letters of inquiry to the University of California Press, a compilation of student-run journals at UC Berkeley and submission information, and a list of questions a student author might ask a prospective publisher.

Both the workshop and the resulting publication are intended to guide students in deciding what and when to publish and thereby to help them complete the dissertation in a timely manner. In other words, the workshop and publication should assist students in becoming successful professionals in the discipline.

Conclusion

Because the Graduate Division at UC Berkeley cares about its graduate students and takes its role as an educational unit seriously, it is committed to supporting all students at every phase of the degree program. Because our research demonstrated that humanities and social science students encounter specific field-specific obstacles to successful completion, especially during the critical dissertation-writing stage, the Graduate Division has implemented programs designed to address the particular needs of humanities and social science students as they write dissertations. By advising departments to allocate student's financial support, providing one-year dissertation fellowships, organizing and leading interdisciplinary dissertation workshops, presenting practical strategies for dissertation writing, and creating resources for academic publishing, the institution has endeavored to expedite the dissertation-writing process.

An analysis of data on doctoral students' progress indicates that our efforts have been successful. Comparing doctoral completion rates over time, we found that, overall, the doctoral completion rate increased by 11 percent (see Table 7.2). This percentage is consistent with the limited comparable national data on retention (Bowen and Rudenstine, 1992; Miselis, McManus, and Kraus, 1991; National Research Council, 1996).

Using a somewhat different time frame in 1997 than in the 1991 Nerad study, one sees that of the cohort entering between 1975 and 1977, 49 percent completed a doctoral degree. Of those who entered from 1978 through 1980, 55 percent received a doctoral degree. Of the cohort who entered between 1981 and 1983, 60 percent completed a doctoral degree.

Comparing the group that entered between 1975 and 1977 with those who entered between 1981 and 1983 yielded the following results. In the arts, the completion rate increased from 37 percent to 44 percent. Likewise, the doctoral completion rates increased in languages and literatures from 27 percent to 43 percent. In the social sciences, the rate went from 43 percent to 52 percent. We like to think that the improved doctoral completion rates for the later entering cohorts in the humanities and social sciences are, to some degree, a result of the Graduate Division's efforts to assist students during the critical dissertation-writing phase of the doctoral program.

In the process, we hope that we have also helped reinvigorate intellectual life and interaction among students and helped create cross-disciplinary intellectual communities. We see evidence that in providing information and model programs, the institution has acted as a catalyst. Students, faculty, and departments are adopting and modifying these programs to fit their specific needs.

Table 7.2. Completion Rates of Doctoral Students at UC Berkeley

Field	1975–1977 (after 11 years)		1978–1980 (after 11 years)		1981–1983 (after 11 years)	
	N	(percent)	N	(percent)	N	(percent)
Arts	82	(37)	74	(36)	91	(44)
Biological sciences	312	(68)	333	(70)	334	(73)
Engineering	679	(53)	727	(63)	746	(65)
Languages and literatures	427	(27)	328	(35)	350	(43)
Natural resources	186	(58)	185	(65)	172	(63)
Physical sciences	770	(63)	754	(67)	741	(73)
Professional schools[a]	637	(40)	650	(39)	467	(48)
Natural social sciences	759	(43)	697	(49)	652	(52)
Total students	3,852	(49)	3,748	(55)	3,553	(60)

Note: N = number of entering students.

Note: Completion rates were calculated eleven years after students enrolled in the graduate school at Berkeley; that means for 1986, 1987, and 1988, respectively.

Note: This table uses a different mode of calculating attrition and somewhat different definitions than the 1991 study, as shown in Table 7.1.

[a] Includes architecture, business administration, city and regional planning, education, librarianship, public health, public policy, and social welfare.

Source: Graduate Division, UC Berkeley, "les7583," Jan. 21, 1997.

MARESI NERAD is director of graduate research in the Graduate Division at the University of California, Berkeley.

DEBRA SANDS MILLER is senior writer in the Graduate Division Research Unit at the University of California, Berkeley.

The recruiting paradigm and employment trends for engineering Ph.D.'s imply that we should shift our efforts to support graduate students through doctoral study. Recruiting and retaining women and minority candidates require a multifaceted approach.

Pursuing the Ph.D. in the Sciences and Engineering: Trends and Observations

Roger E. Salters

Historically, the road to the Ph.D. degree in the sciences and engineering has been paved with good intentions, and those who travel it have been assured a high level of success. Before the 1980s, the paradigm for recruiting, training, and employing the successful science and engineering Ph.D. student was rather standard: locate the best male Bachelor of Science (B.S.) student graduating from one of the top twenty research institutions, offer him a very good research assistantship for several years, and then wait for this top-notch researcher to emerge from one of the outstanding research-intensive institutions so that he can take his well-deserved academic position in such an institution.

This road map appeared to have worked quite well for the physical sciences until the early 1970s, when the number of international students pursuing physical science Ph.D.'s at U.S. universities increased (Holden, 1995). Later, employment opportunities from foreign countries for students with baccalaureate and master's degrees began having a competitive impact on the growth of doctoral engineering programs in the United States. According to some, this demand has not even crested yet. This high international demand for science and engineering Ph.D.'s led the National Science Foundation (NSF) to "trigger alarms about a Ph.D. shortfall predicted" for the early twenty-first century, "even though Ph.D. production was growing from about 19,000 a year between 1976 and 1986 to 25,000 in 1993" (Holden, 1995, pp. 123–125).

The 1980s also brought another challenge to the old paradigm of producing new Ph.D.'s in science and engineering. This challenge was staged from within the borders of the country, for in 1983, women received about 25 percent of the Ph.D. degrees awarded in science and engineering that year (Magner, 1996). By 1993, women earned about 30 percent of the science and engineering Ph.D.'s. This increased to 31 percent by 1995 (Magner, 1996). Indications are that this trend will continue.

In the late 1980s, a record number of underrepresented minorities received Ph.D.'s, which further strained the old paradigm. In this category, which includes African Americans, Hispanic Americans, Native Americans, and persons with disabilities, these numbers are still quite small, but the trend shows potential for significant growth in the next century.

In the following sections, I shall present some details of how academe, industry, and government are changing the old paradigm for producing Ph.D. recipients in science and engineering. I shall also discuss how employment is changing for these graduates and what institutions are doing to encourage persons of color to enter the sciences and engineering.

The Changing Candidate Pool

The pool of candidates entering graduate education has indeed changed, especially in terms of their undergraduate backgrounds. According to the *NSF Special Report* (National Science Foundation, 1992), Ph.D. graduates in science reported the following origins for their baccalaureate degrees:

Type of Institution	Students from Such Schools
Specialized institutions	1 percent
Liberal arts institutions	15 percent
Comprehensive universities	21 percent
Other doctorate-granting universities	25 percent
Research-intensive universities	38 percent

Engineering doctorate recipients provided the following information about their backgrounds:

Type of Institution	Students from Such Schools
Specialized institutions	4 percent
Liberal arts institutions	4 percent
Other doctorate-granting universities	28 percent
Research-intensive universities	53 percent

Given the backgrounds of both those entering and those graduating, research universities play a major role in educating science and engineering doctorates.

Yet heretofore underrepresented groups, such as women and people of color, who entered these degree programs came from different institutions of higher learning. Furthermore, women are becoming a progressively larger percentage of the Ph.D. recipients who did their undergraduate work at liberal arts institutions. In 1991, approximately 18 percent of liberal arts graduates who went on to receive Ph.D.'s in science or engineering were female, while 12 percent were male. About 19 percent of African American science or engineering Ph.D. recipients received their undergraduate degrees from liberal arts institutions. Fourteen percent of whites, 10 percent of Asians, and 7 percent of Hispanic Americans and Native Americans received baccalaureate degrees from such institutions (Washington, 1993).

For African American students, the Historically Black Colleges and Universities (HBCUs) continue to play an important role in undergraduate education despite the growth of diversity on campuses across the nation (National Science Foundation, 1996). In 1993, approximately 30 percent of all African Americans receiving bachelor's degrees in science and engineering graduated from an HBCU. The master's degree is the usual entry level into doctoral programs in science and engineering. That is, the B.S. degree recipient will first earn a master's degree and then enter a Ph.D. program. In engineering, however, because there is a terminal master's degree that leads to most employment opportunities, minority students frequently choose to attain that degree rather than going on for the doctorate. For this reason, there has been only a modest increase in the percentage of minorities in science and engineering doctoral programs since 1985. For example, in 1993, of the 14,913 recipients of science and engineering doctorates, there were 374 African Americans, 446 Hispanic Americans, and 43 Native Americans (National Science Foundation, 1996, p. 210). These numbers are still quite small.

To maintain an adequate pool of graduate student candidates and to nurture those candidates into the doctoral level, the new Ph.D. paradigm must assist students more proactively to encourage greater learning and training through all levels, from undergraduate to doctoral programs. Recent information from the American Council on Education and the *NSF Report* (National Science Foundation, 1996) gave the following disturbing attrition figure for all undergraduate students: approximately 36 percent for African Americans; 22 percent Hispanic Americans, 12 percent for Native Americans, and 8 percent for whites. Given that the enrollment figures for minority groups in undergraduate science and engineering were quite small initially, the relatively large attrition percentages strongly indicate why the eventual Ph.D. recipient numbers are very small for minorities.

The changes in the Ph.D. candidate pool, as reflected in the varied institutions for candidates' initial training and education as well as their shifting demographics, are not the only reasons we need a new paradigm. We must also revise the methods of educating, training, and supporting these candidates while they are in doctoral programs. I will address these latter concerns next.

The Changing Ways of Financing Graduate Schools

Financing graduate education, regardless of the student's gender or ethnicity, is crucial to the candidate's success. From the 1960s through the 1980s when the cold war raged, the U.S. government's funding for engineering research provided vast opportunities for research assistantships at most of the research-intensive universities. Then, after President Kennedy mandated that we put a man on the moon before the end of the 1960s, the National Aeronautics and Space Administration (NASA) spent record amounts in many areas of the aerospace industry, including engineering departments at research-intensive universities. The weapon systems buildup during the Vietnam War and the Soviet threat motivated the Department of Defense to fund research into weapons systems and related support areas quite heavily.

For the physical sciences, however, the research funding pool appeared to have decreased long before the 1960s (Holden, 1995). According to some sources, "Policies for graduate education, particularly in science and engineering, have not been seriously considered since the end of World War II" (Holden, 1995, p. 121). This is probably truer for the sciences than for engineering.

Today's trend is somewhat different, because teaching assistantships also play a significant role as a means for funding graduate school at the doctoral level. *NSF Report 96–311* indicates that approximately 12 percent of male graduate students and 13 percent of female graduate students support themselves primarily through teaching assistantships. These numbers are a bit misleading in that 12 percent of males means 17,646 men, whereas 13 percent of females means 7,537 women. According to the report, proportionally more men than women receive most of their funding through research assistantships. I shall comment on this later.

When disability, race or ethnicity, and citizenship status are accounted for, the award of both teaching and research assistantships varies. There appear to be fewer awards given to these categories of graduate students. Doctoral students with disabilities received financial aid and need-based aid about as often as others did. Some U.S. citizens who were from a racial or ethnic minority and who received science and engineering doctorates were more likely than others to cite assistantships as their major support. Assistantships went to 11 percent of white students compared with 10 percent of Native Americans, 9 percent of Hispanic Americans, 8 percent of Asians, and 6 percent of African Americans. The NSF study cited research assistantships as the primary support for 32 percent of Asians, 23 percent of whites, 17 percent of Hispanic Americans, 15 percent of Native Americans, and 9 percent of African Americans earning doctorates in science and engineering.

Again, we must remind ourselves that the base numbers on which the above percentages are calculated differ greatly. That is, the top fifty institutions enrolled 332,525 U.S. citizens as graduate students in science and engineering in 1993. There were 17,181 African Americans, 1,318 Native Americans, 13,446 Hispanic Americans, 24,401 Asian Americans, 258,278 whites, and some students listed as other or unknown (National Science Foundation, 1996).

The Changing Employment of Ph.D. Recipients

The *Graduating Engineer* ("Directory of Engineering Employment," 1996) gives some interesting statistics about the employment of engineers from the standpoint of research and development, salaries, characteristics needed to succeed in the workplace, and trends in employment opportunities. These data show that companies are trying to make themselves attractive to engineers with bachelor's degrees who may want to pursue graduate degrees. This process thus produced high employment for engineers in the last decade. According to the Bureau of Labor Statistics ("Directory of Engineering Employment," 1996), the unemployment rate for engineers had declined from about 4 percent at the end of 1991 to around 1.5 percent during the first quarter of 1996.

Now that so many companies have given jobs to vast numbers of engineers with baccalaureate degrees, industry is developing innovative methods and programs to provide continuing on-line education to these engineers via remote classroom technologies (Thomas, 1996, 1997). Many of the top research-intensive universities provide such on-line programs to advanced degrees. This trend suggests that the twenty-first century will usher in a larger number of part-time Ph.D. students, which further reflects a need for a paradigm shift in the Ph.D. recipient pipeline.

This vast employment of engineers with B.S. degrees and industry's need for advanced knowledge have stimulated debates within academe that the first professional engineering degree should be the master's or even the doctorate. Friedland and Dorato (1987) and Dorato (1994) make this case very convincingly. To support his position, Dorato (1994) lists several key reasons that there is inadequate time in the standard B.S. curriculum to build sufficiently broad and deep knowledge so that the engineer can function in the workplace. Dorato, however, does not cite technical knowledge so much as interpersonal abilities that an engineer needs in order to fit into the industrial job. These skills are not essential for studies toward the Ph.D., but they are natural consequences of the Ph.D. process. These observations of Dorato's are consistent with the aforementioned trends identified in *NSF Report* (National Science Foundation, 1996) for 1993.

If efforts to make the graduate degree the first professional degree in engineering are successful, then the greater demand for graduate education will further tax the resources of academic institutions. The delay in moving students into industry will decrease employment levels. This in turn will place a greater demand on the number of Ph.D.'s required in academe to meet the increased research and teaching needs. This multidimensional drain on the advanced degree recipients will, however, open up more opportunities for underrepresented minorities and women to secure tenure-track faculty positions at institutions that award graduate degrees in engineering. There should be fewer people competing for these positions. Industry also will contribute to this new paradigm by offering greater support to the graduate student and to universities' research laboratories, where research will be more product-focused. As a consequence of these changes in the production of master's and Ph.D. degrees in engineering, there will be corresponding changes in the graduate programs of the sciences. That is, as engineering pushes the envelope of available science to support technology, there must also be a steady growth in science Ph.D. programs.

This partnership between academe and industry to provide graduate-level educational opportunities to a larger pool of B.S. engineering graduates represents a win-win situation for all involved. The students will benefit from the new paradigm because women and underrepresented minorities will have greater access to graduate education. This access means that there should be more tenure-track faculty positions in science and engineering at the various Ph.D.-granting institutions. In addition, academic institutions will benefit from increased revenues that they will receive through research grants sponsored by industry and the government. Finally, industry will benefit from the larger pool of qualified science and engineering talent and from the additional research and development component available through their sponsored programs.

Changing Methods to Attract Underrepresented Students

I conclude this chapter by making a few comments on current initiatives being taken to increase the number of women and minorities in the science and engineering pipeline. First, NASA has taken some very bold steps toward increasing the number of undergraduate students in science and engineering graduate schools by funding university research centers at several minority institutions. These centers provide work-study and undergraduate research assistantships to undergraduate students. They also provide graduate research assistantships at both the master's and Ph.D. levels. These centers for minority master's and Ph.D. degree recipients have very ambitious production goals; for example, the Autonomous Control Engineering Center at the University of New Mexico seeks to graduate fifty master's and Ph.D. minority students in engineering within five years.

Second, the School of Engineering at Stanford University has a very aggressive program called "Recruitment of Targeted Minorities." This program is for M.S. and Ph.D. students in nine engineering areas and is administered by an associate dean. This level of administration demonstrates the commitment of Stanford University to the need for such initiatives. The Stanford program has been quite effective, as the following outcomes illustrate. From 1984 to 1989, an average of 24 targeted minority students received graduate engineering degrees each year; however, from 1990 to 1996, this number grew to over 50. In 1996, 190 targeted minority students enrolled in the Stanford program, with 60 of these entering the Ph.D. programs. These results are encouraging.

Finally, organizations such as the National Action Council for Minorities in Engineering, Inc., the Society for the Advancement of Chicanos and Native Americans in Science, the National Association of Minority Engineering Program Administrators, and others have taken very active roles to increase the number of minority students in graduate science and engineering programs. These organizations have implemented special science programs for student in kindergarten through seventh grade; science fairs, design contests, and mentoring for eighth through twelfth graders; and college-level programs to provide mentoring and scholarship support. On average, these targeted efforts show 2 to 5 percent increases in the number of minority students enrolling in science and engineering at colleges and universities. The number of Hispanic American males and Native American males is declining, however, and this trend requires urgent attention.

Summary

In this chapter, I have provided trends and observations about the old paradigm of producing Ph.D. recipients in the sciences and engineering. I have included factual statistics, as well as speculations by some pioneers of academic change. These form the bases for a new paradigm for producing the Ph.D.'s in the sciences and engineering into the twenty-first century. Finally, I have considered the multidimensional nature of the new paradigm, and have discussed some current efforts to increase the number of minority engineering students in the graduate school pipeline.

ROGER E. SALTERS is associate professor of engineering at the University of Denver, where he also serves as the adviser to the student chapters of the National Association of Black Engineers and the National Association of Hispanic Engineers. He is also a member of the National Association of Minority Engineering Programs Directors and is on the Board of Directors of the Colorado Minority Engineering Association.

The contributions to this volume are considered within the general context of the stages of students' graduate careers, previous research on degree completion, and an analysis of the tasks involved in completing the dissertation.

Completing the Dissertation: Theory, Research, and Practice

Leonard L. Baird

Although the forms and to some degree the meaning of the dissertation have changed since the last century (Berelson, 1960; Council of Graduate Schools, 1991; Goodchild and Miller, Chapter Two of this volume), writing a dissertation is still generally considered an intellectual challenge and sometimes a problematic task. As Nerad and Miller state in Chapter Seven of this volume, dissertation authors must deal with "questions about originality, the importance of the subject matter, the dissertation's scope, and the form of the dissertation."

Of course, the nature of the dissertation varies by discipline. In history, for example, a student's dissertation is often expected to be his or her first book and to contribute to knowledge and thus may require years to complete. In contrast, in some science fields, a dissertation may be an assemblage of articles to which the student has contributed an introduction, a review of the literature, some new information, and a conclusion (Lipschutz, 1993). Even within departments, faculty may not entirely agree about the dissertation (Isaac, Quinlan, and Walker, 1992). Moreover, changing student clienteles, as described for the sciences and engineering in Chapter Eight, for example, requires new attention to different learning styles. In short, the completion of a dissertation can be a formidable and complex task, for student and faculty alike.

The contributors to this volume demonstrate, in different ways, the complexity of the dissertation process. In this chapter, I shall attempt to place the individual chapters into a general context by considering the stages of the academic career, summarizing the research that bears on dissertation completion, reviewing the tasks involved in completing a dissertation, and considering some of the implications for programs and faculty.

NEW DIRECTIONS FOR HIGHER EDUCATION, no. 99, Fall 1997 © Jossey-Bass Publishers

The Stages of the Graduate Student Career

Graduate education has been described as a process of becoming socialized into an ultimate professional role (Baird, 1990b; Stein and Weidman, 1990). This process involves learning the "specialized knowledge, skills, attitudes, values, norms, and interests of the profession" (Bragg, 1976, p. 1). The graduate faculty members are the critical agents conducting this socialization, because they define knowledge and disciplinary values, model the roles of academics in the discipline, and give practical help and advice (Stein and Weidman, 1990). Graduate student peers are the other socializing agents (Baird, 1990b, 1993; Tinto, 1991), although this group is seldom given formal recognition. Thus socialization at the graduate level would appear to involve academic and social integration processes similar to those at the undergraduate level (Tinto, 1987, 1991).

These concepts have a different meaning at the graduate level and vary with the stages of the academic career (Baird, 1972, 1990b, 1993; Katz, 1976; Tinto, 1991). Because the various stages of the graduate career present different tasks and demands, students' relations with faculty and other students also differ. At the beginning of graduate programs, students are still learning the expectations and demands of the discipline and are therefore somewhat distant from faculty. At this stage, students may see their peers as unknown quantities or as competitors. As students progress through graduate programs, they ideally become integrated into their institutions, departments, and disciplines. This assimilation to the discipline's norms and methods gives them more access to faculty, with whom they can have more interactions, especially at the thesis or dissertation stage (Baird, 1972, 1993; Tinto, 1991). They also begin to view their peers as part of a departmental community (Baird, 1990b, 1993; Lozoff, 1976).

Research That Bears on Dissertation Completion

Studies of degree completion and time-to-degree in graduate education suggest that a number of variables are important (Baird, 1990a; Berelson, 1960; Bowen and Rudenstine, 1992; Girves and Wemmerus, 1988; Gunn and Sanford, 1988; Tuckman, Coyle, and Bae, 1990; Wilson, 1965). Several of these variables concern decisions made prior to entry, such as delayed entrance to graduate school (perhaps as a result of other responsibilities or of less intense interest). Some factors in attrition and time-to-degree involve students' employment situation, whether that includes full-time work outside the university, assistantships or fellowships inside the department, or full- or part-time attendance. (A lower attendance status prevents students from meeting requirements as quickly and increases the likelihood that other responsibilities will compete for students' energies.) Likewise, both marriage and children tend to create delays or end progress toward the degree, especially for women.

At the department level, students appear more likely to complete their degrees in departments with the following characteristics.

- They have coherent, well-planned programs and regular procedures for monitoring students' progress.
- They use the resources available to fund as many students as possible through a mixture of assistantships, fellowships, grants, and loans.
- They help students identify dissertation topics early in their programs.
- They create ample opportunities for informal interaction among students and between faculty and students.

Disciplines clearly differ. Time-to-degree is shortest in the bench sciences, such as chemistry, and the mathematical disciplines. It takes longer to receive a Ph.D. in the social sciences and the longest time in the humanities. The difference in average time-to-doctorate between the fastest and slowest disciplines is four years (Baird, 1990a). All these factors could be examined in isolation but can be better understood as part of the process of doctoral education.

The Dissertation Stage

As described earlier, graduate education leading to the doctorate is a fairly lengthy process of becoming socialized in the field. Ideally, students will reach the dissertation stage with a clear conception of their interests, a viable prospective dissertation topic, and an arsenal of knowledge and skills that they can use when working on the dissertation (Council of Graduate Schools, 1990). Sometimes, however, students have not successfully negotiated this process, despite completing the course work and examinations. They may have poor relationships with professors and fellow students, inadequate mastery of the forms of reasoning favored by the discipline, and little support from spouses, employers, and other groups.

Sometimes the program (as opposed to the student) is not well organized to ensure degree completion. That is, programs that do not make an effort to integrate students socially and academically into the department, that are not clear about the courses and experiences that will give students mastery of the discipline's methods and language, and that do not carefully monitor students' progress will have high numbers of ABD students. In short, whether due to personal choices or departmental practices, students can arrive at the dissertation stage at different levels of readiness for the task.

It may help to consider the nature of that task (Council of Graduate Schools, 1991). As I tell my own students, writing a dissertation is like no other writing they have done before and like none they will do later. The dissertation is a unique intellectual and practical enterprise, as has been outlined in many guides. It requires several elements:

An idea
A method
A committee
Advice and guidance
Finances
Familiarity with the process and its forms
A peer group
Encouragement

An Idea. As obvious as it seems that students need an idea, this is a sticking point for many. They have difficulty in formulating a question to investigate. Ideally, this question would flow fairly naturally out of course work, but it often does not. Students sometimes see course work and dissertations as separate. To remedy this, courses should emphasize research and should require students to do as much research as possible on ideas that stimulate them, as Kluever suggests in Chapter Four. Likewise, advisers should encourage students early on to begin considering possible dissertation ideas. Through his or her own work, an adviser should demonstrate the excitement and pleasure that research can bring.

A Method. It is also obvious that students need a method of investigation, and all programs attempt to provide their students with research skills. As with course work, however, students sometimes do not see the relevance of research courses for the dissertation. Again, students should be required to do research, not just to learn about methods. This procedure can make the transition to dissertation topics much easier. In addition, as Creswell and Miller suggest in Chapter Three, students can find a methodology that meets their needs and can take appropriate courses. As there may be some lapse of time between research courses and the dissertation, mini-courses in particular methods might be given for advanced students.

A Committee. One of the critical tasks for dissertation students is choosing faculty to serve as committee members. The adviser should make sure that students understand the committee's functions and purpose. Ideally, the committee will help students move through the dissertation. The committee member should be seen as a resource, not a gatekeeper. The adviser's knowledge of the field and the faculty in the program can be invaluable in the selection process. For example, the adviser may know that a professor's own research is primarily quantitative but that she is, nevertheless, quite sympathetic to qualitative research. Likewise, fellow students may have helpful perspectives on choosing committee members.

Advice and Guidance. Since the dissertation is such a major project, students need advice and guidance throughout the dissertation process. The adviser is, of course, the main person to assist in this area, so regular meetings should be scheduled with the adviser. Research is an interactive process in which people seek others' help to get the job done; the adviser should emphasize this point.

The adviser is not the only person who can offer assistance, however. Committees in some fields include a methodological expert. Professors are sometimes included on committees for their particular intellectual perspective. Procedures that ensure regular contact with these professors, both individually and in groupings, could be most helpful.

Other students can also provide information and guidance. Groups of students with similar interests can help each other hone ideas, locate resources, and suggest strategies for coping with professors and the bureaucracy, as Nerad and Miller suggest in Chapter Seven. Students should be encouraged to cope with the demands of completing the dissertation both formally and informally.

Finances. Programs may have relatively few resources to help students, as Lenz suggests in Chapter Six. The adviser and the program should know about the institutional and other resources available, however, and should attempt to connect students with them. Perhaps a particular professor in the department could be asked to locate and disseminate information about these sources—with some release time from other duties, of course.

Familiarity with the Process and Its Forms. Some students pass through graduate school in a kind of haze, never sure about what is required or expected. This is particularly true at the dissertation stage. Obviously, it is in the best interests of both students and programs to be clear about the procedures, forms, and standards required. Institutions could prepare checklists of formal requirements, distribute statements of expected standards, and offer courses on preparing dissertations. They could even make videotapes showing a staged meeting in which the dissertation is approved, meetings with advisers, and the final oral defense, because students often have great anxiety and several misconceptions about these milestones. Nerad and Miller offer many additional suggestions in Chapter Seven.

A Peer Group. Students need to feel at home in a program, and the other students are critical to creating this comfort. Although individual faculty can play a small role in this acclimatization by introducing students with similar interests, the program can exert much more influence by providing and promoting formal and informal gatherings for dissertation-level students. In particular, if students just beginning their dissertations can mingle with more seasoned candidates, they can receive information about the process and the psychological changes it will engender. In addition, more advanced students can "model" the behavior, strategies, and approaches the less advanced student will need to master. Additional ideas may be found in Nerad and Miller's suggestions in Chapter Seven.

Encouragement. Dissertations can take years to write and are rarely completed in less than one year. The length and difficulty of the task provide ample reasons for discouragement, and even the most positive student can be tempted to quit. Faculty who regularly see their advisees can help them over these rough spots, which is another reason for routine meetings. Groups of students can help each other cope with discouragement. Again, this is easier to do if their interactions are regular.

Thus, we can do much to help students complete their dissertations, although the program cannot do everything. A lot of responsibility falls on the student. Still, numerous studies (see Baird, 1990b) point to areas in which programs can and should help, and I believe graduate educators have a responsibility to intervene productively.

Roles for Programs and Faculty

Although the program's official responsibility is to be chiefly concerned with academic matters while students pursue their studies, advisers play additional roles, both during the course of studies and afterward. One such role is that of mentor. Although *mentoring* has many meanings and is sometimes ill defined (Merriam, 1983), it almost certainly means providing career advice, understanding the role to which the protégé aspires, possessing specific field-relevant expertise, endorsing the student's work to others in the field, and collaborating (Busch, 1985; Sands, Parson, and Duane, 1991). Mentoring is especially critical as students are about to embark on their professional careers (Tierney and Rhoads, 1993).

In addition, faculty members form professional relationships with students that often develop into strong personal relationships. Since faculty-student contacts involve many aspects of students' lives (course scheduling, finances, working around students' other commitments), faculty members, particularly advisers, come to know students as people. Usually, these relationships proceed in an amicable and beneficial way. As studies (Heinrich, 1991, 1995) have shown, however, these relationships can sometimes be manipulative, uncaring, and confrontational. The ethical adviser will be careful not to fall into any of these patterns. Even when the relationship is proceeding well, there are continuous issues about the appropriate degree of involvement, dependence, and sometimes unconscious manipulation (Baird, 1990b). Advisers need to be aware of these possibilities.

With their knowledge of the field, faculty members can help students immensely by seeking employment opportunities for their advisees and letting students know about these opportunities. In many ways, a faculty member can be a career adviser, as well as an academic one. This means reviewing students' goals, interests, and priorities. Many fields have a limited supply of traditional academic positions. Faculty should seek out information about alternative careers in business, government, or other levels of education in order to be able to give the best career advice possible.

A final role for the faculty member needs to be mentioned—that of the exemplar or inspirer. By being someone who attempts to produce the highest quality of work, the adviser can convey a vision of the true professional. By calling upon the student to have the same aspirations, the adviser can inspire students to seek the highest levels of performance of which they are capable. When the adviser inspires the student to perform at a high professional level, and when others recognize the student's excellence through the quality of their publications or through their accomplishments as practicing professionals, these successes reflect well on the adviser (Isaac, Quinlan, and Walker, 1992).

Completing the Dissertation: The Nexus of Responsibility

The contributors to this volume suggest that completing a dissertation is a complex task, involving responsibilities for both programs and students. As I have argued in this chapter, programs bear major obligations to have clear requirements. Programs should provide good advising, help students begin focusing on a dissertation topic early in their studies, provide as much appropriate financial assistance as possible, provide opportunities for research experiences, help students form dissertation groups, and eliminate as much red tape from the process as they can. Students also have obligations to begin thinking about a dissertation early on, get to know faculty members early on who may serve on their committees, be sure they understand requirements and expectations, and determine the priority they wish to place the dissertation in their lives.

Although one might consider these institutional and student obligations as separate, it is more productive to think of them as mutual, as providing opportunities for collaboration and creativity. By working together, faculty and students can increase the chances that students will complete their dissertations. In putting joint energy toward this goal, faculty and students will gain mutual respect and understanding.

LEONARD L. BAIRD is professor of higher education in the Higher Education and Student Affairs Program at Ohio State University. He is also editor of the Journal of Higher Education.

REFERENCES

Abedi, J., and Benkin, E. "The Effects of Students' Academic, Financial, and Demographic Variables on Time to the Doctorate." *Research in Higher Education,* 1987, *27,* 3–14.

Aitken, M. E. "A Personality Profile of the College Student Procrastinator." Ph.D. diss., University of Pittsburgh, 1982. Abstract in *Dissertation Abstracts International,* 1982, *43* (03), 722A.

Atkinson, C. *True Confessions of a Ph.D.* Boston: Meador, 1939.

Atwell, R. H. "Doctoral Education Must Match the Nation's Needs and the Realities of the Marketplace." *Chronicle of Higher Education,* Nov. 29, 1996, B4–5.

Baird, L. L. "The Relation of Graduate Students' Role Relations to Their Stage of Academic Career, Employment, and Academic Success." *Organizational Behavior and Human Performance,* 1972, *7,* 428–441.

Baird, L. L. "Disciplines and Doctorates: The Relationships Between Program Characteristics and the Duration of Doctoral Study." *Research in Higher Education,* 1990a, *31,* 369–385.

Baird, L. L. "The Melancholy of Anatomy: The Personal and Professional Development of Graduate and Professional School Students." In J. C. Smart (ed.), *Higher Education: Handbook of Theory and Research.* Vol. 6. New York: Agathon Press, 1990b.

Baird, L. L. "Using Research and Theoretical Models of Graduate Student Progress." In L. L. Baird (ed.), *Increasing Graduate Student Retention and Degree Attainment.* San Francisco: Jossey-Bass, 1993.

Barrow, J. C., and Moore, C. A. "Group Interventions with Perfectionistic Thinking." *Personnel and Guidance Journal,* 1983, *62,* 612–615.

Benkin, E. M. "Where Have All the Doctoral Students Gone? A Study of Doctoral Student Attrition at UCLA." Ph.D. diss., University of California, Los Angeles, 1984. Abstract in *Dissertation Abstracts International,* 1985, *45* (09), 2770A.

Berelson, B. *Graduate Education in the United States.* New York: McGraw-Hill, 1960.

Bloland, H. G. "Postmodernism and Higher Education." *Journal of Higher Education,* 1995, *66* (5), 521–559.

Bogdan, R. C., and Biklen, S. K. *Qualitative Research for Education: An Introduction to Theory and Methods.* (2nd ed.) Needham Heights, Mass.: Allyn & Bacon, 1992.

Bowen, W. G., and Rudenstine, N. L. *In Pursuit of the Ph.D.* Princeton, N.J.: Princeton University Press, 1992.

Bradley, B. W. (ed.).*The Graduate Handbook, no. 7, 1899.* Philadelphia: Lippincott, 1899.

Bragg, A. K. *The Socialization Process in Higher Education.* ERIC/Higher Education Research Report no. 7. Washington, D.C.: American Association for Higher Education, 1976. (ED 132 909)

Breneman, D. W. *The Ph.D. Degree at Berkeley: Interviews, Placement, and Recommendations.* Berkeley: Office of the Vice President–Planning, University of California, 1971.

Brewer, J., and Hunter, A. *Multimethod Research: A Synthesis of Styles.* Thousand Oaks, Calif.: Sage, 1989.

Brubacher, J. S., and Rudy, W. *Higher Education in Transition: A History of American Colleges and Universities, 1636–1968.* New York: HarperCollins, 1968.

Burka, J. B., and Yuen, L. M. *Procrastination: Why You Do It, What to Do About It.* Reading, Mass.: Addison-Wesley, 1983.

Burrell, G., and Morgan, G. *Sociological Paradigms and Organizational Analysis.* London and Portsmouth, N.H.: Heinemann, 1979.

Busch, J. W. "Mentoring in Graduate Schools of Education: Mentors' Perceptions." *American Educational Research Journal,* 1985, *22,* 256–265.

Carmichael, O. C. *Graduate Education: A Critique and a Program.* New York: HarperCollins, 1961.

Carnegie Foundation for the Advancement of Teaching. *A Classification of Institutions of Higher Education.* Princeton, N.J.: Carnegie Foundation, 1994.

Cesari, J. P. "Thesis and Dissertation Support Groups: A Unique Service for Graduate Students." *Journal of College Student Development,* 1990, *31,* 375–376.

Chodorow, N. "Family Structure and Feminine Personality." In M. Z. Rosaldo and L. Lamphere (eds.), *Woman, Culture, and Society.* Stanford, Calif.: Stanford University Press, 1974.

Clifford, G. J., and Guthrie, J. W. *Ed School.* Chicago: University of Chicago Press, 1988.

Cone, J. D., and Foster, S. L. *Dissertations and Theses from Start to Finish.* Washington, D.C.: American Psychological Association, 1993.

Conference Board of Associated Research Councils. *An Assessment of Research Doctorate Programs in the United States.* 5 vols. Washington, D.C.: National Academy Press, 1982.

Cordasco, F. *The Shaping of American Graduate Education: Daniel Coit Gilman and the Protean Ph.D.* Lanham, Md.: Rowman & Littlefield, 1973. (Originally published 1959.)

Council of Graduate Schools. *The Doctor of Philosophy Degree.* Washington, D.C.: Council of Graduate Schools, 1990.

Council of Graduate Schools. *The Role and Nature of the Doctoral Dissertation: A Policy Statement.* Washington, D.C.: Council of Graduate Schools, 1991.

Creswell, J. W. *Research Design: Qualitative and Quantitative Approaches.* Thousand Oaks, Calif.: Sage, 1994.

Creswell, J. W. "Composing a Mixed Method Study." Paper presented at the annual meeting of the American Educational Research Association, Chicago, Mar. 1997a.

Creswell, J. W. *Qualitative Inquiry and Research Design: Choosing Among Five Traditions.* Thousand Oaks, Calif.: Sage, 1997b.

Creswell, J. W., and Brown, M. L. "How Chairpersons Enhance Faculty Research: A Grounded Theory Study." *Review of Higher Education,* 1992, *16* (1), 41–62.

Creswell, J. W., Goodchild, L. F., and Turner, P. P. "Integrated Qualitative and Quantitative Research: Epistemology, History, and Designs." In J. C. Smart (ed.), *Higher Education: Handbook of Theory and Research.* Vol. 11. New York: Agathon Press, 1996.

Cunningham, J. W., and Fitzgerald, J. "Epistemology and Reading." *Reading Research Quarterly,* 1996, *31* (1), 36–60.

Davis, G. B., and Parker, C. A. *Writing the Doctoral Dissertation: A Systematic Approach.* Hauppauge, N.Y.: Barron's Educational Series, 1979.

Denzin, N. K. *Interpretive Biography.* Thousand Oaks, Calif.: Sage, 1989.

Dickens, C. S. "Collaboration in the Research and Scholarship of Feminist Women Faculty." Paper presented at the annual meeting of the Association for the Study of Higher Education, Pittsburgh, Nov. 1993.

Digest of Education Statistics (U.S. Department of Education NCES 92–097). Washington, D.C.: U.S. Government Printing Office, 1992.

Digest of Education Statistics (U.S. Department of Education NCES 96–133). Washington, D.C.: U.S. Government Printing Office, 1996.

"Directory of Engineering Employment." *Graduating Engineer,* 1996, *17* (2), 12–27.

Dorato, P. "First Professional Engineering Degree: Graduate or Undergraduate?" *Bent of Tau Beta Pi,* fall 1994, pp. 10–11.

Dulles, E. L. *Eleanor Lansing Dulles: Change of a Lifetime: A Memoir.* Upper Saddle River, N.J.: Prentice Hall, 1980.

Eliot, C. W. Letter to Daniel Coit Gilman, Oct. 20, 1897. Daniel Coit Gilman Papers, Correspondence Collection, box: E, file: Eliot, Charles W. (1886–). Ferdinand Hamburger, Jr. Archives (hereafter cited as FHA), Johns Hopkins University, Baltimore.

Ellis, A., and Knaus, W. J. *Overcoming Procrastination.* New York: NAL/Dutton, 1977.

Engleman, F. E. *The Pleasure Was Mine: Seventy Years in Education.* Danville, Ill.: Interstate, 1971.

Flett, G. L., Blankstein, K. R., Hewitt, P. L., and Koledin, S. "Components of Perfectionism and Procrastination in College Students." *Social Behavior and Personality,* 1992, *20,* 85–94.

Flexner, A. *I Remember: The Autobiography of Abraham Flexner.* New York: Simon & Schuster, 1940.

Franek, S. A. "Counseling Interventions to Facilitate Dissertation Completion." Ph.D. diss., University of Nebraska, 1983. Abstract in *Dissertation Abstracts International,* 1982, *43* (06), 1977B.

Frankena, W. K. *The Philosophy and Future of Graduate Education.* Ann Arbor: University of Michigan Press, 1978.

Fresques, M. T. "Correlational Relationships Among Perfectionism, Achievement Motivation, and Neuroticism." Ph.D. diss., University of Texas, Austin, 1991. Abstract in *Dissertations Abstracts International,* 1991, *53* (3), 1639B.

Friedland, B., and Dorato, P. "A Case for the Doctor of Engineering as a First Professional Degree." *Engineering Education,* Apr.–May 1987, pp. 707–713.

Frost, R. O., Marten, P. A., Lahart, C., and Rosenblate, R. "The Dimensions of Perfectionism." *Cognitive Therapy and Research,* 1990, *14,* 449–468.

Garcia, T., Matula, J. S., Harris, C. L., Egan-Dowdy, K., Lissi, M. R., and Davila, C. "Worriers and Procrastinators: Differences in Motivation, Cognitive Engagement, and Achievement Between Defensive Pessimists and Self-Handicappers." Paper presented at the annual meeting of the American Educational Research Association, San Francisco, Apr. 1995.

Geiger, R. L. *To Advance Knowledge: The Growth of American Research Universities, 1900–1940.* New York: Oxford University Press, 1986.

Geiger, R. L. *Research and Relevant Knowledge: American Research Universities Since World War II.* New York: Oxford University Press, 1993.

Germeroth, D. "Lonely Days and Lonely Nights: Completing the Doctoral Dissertation." *American Communication Association Bulletin,* 1991, *76,* 60–89.

Gildersleeve, V. C. *Many a Good Crusade: Memoirs.* Old Tappan, N.J.: Macmillan, 1954.

Gilligan, C. *In a Different Voice: Psychological Theory and Women's Development.* Cambridge, Mass.: Harvard University Press, 1982.

Gilman, D. C. Letters to J[ohns] H[opkins] T[rustees], Jan. 30, 1875, and Sept. 13, 1875. Daniel Coit Gilman Papers, Collection no. 1, box: Miscellaneous, 1839–1879, file: Outgoing Letters, 1875. FHA, Johns Hopkins University.

Gilman, D. C. "An Address Before the Phi Beta Kappa Society of Harvard University," July 1, 1886. Daniel Coit Gilman Papers, Collection no. 5: Publications, box 5.1: Bibliography of Gilman Speeches and Articles, 1853–1907. FHA, Johns Hopkins University.

Gilman, D. C. *University Problems in the United States.* New York: Century, 1898.

Girves, J. E., and Wemmerus, V. "Developing Models of Graduate Student Degree Progress." *Journal of Higher Education,* 1988, *59,* 163–189.

Gladieux, L. E., Hauptman, A. M., and Knapp, L. G. "The Federal Government and Higher Education." In P. G. Altbach, R. O. Berdahl, and P. J. Gumport (eds.), *Higher Education in American Society.* (3rd ed.) Amherst, N.Y.: Prometheus Books, 1994.

Gleason, P. *Contending with Modernity: Catholic Higher Education in the Twentieth Century.* New York: Oxford University Press, 1995.

Glesne, C., and Peshkin, A. *Becoming Qualitative Researchers: An Introduction.* White Plains, N.Y.: Longman, 1992.

Goddard Library. *The Clark Ph.D.: The First Century, 1891–1981.* Worcester, Mass.: Clark University, 1991.

Goodchild, L. F. "G. Stanley Hall and the Study of Higher Education." *Review of Higher Education,* 1996, *20* (1), 69–99.

Goodspeed, T. W. *A History of the University of Chicago: The First Quarter Century.* Chicago: University of Chicago Press, 1916.

Gordon, L. D. *Gender and Higher Education in the Progressive Era.* New Haven, Conn.: Yale University Press, 1990.

Greene, J. C., Caracelli, V. J., and Graham, W. F. "Toward a Conceptual Framework for Mixed-Method Evaluation Designs." *Educational Evaluation and Policy Analysis,* 1989, *11* (3), 255–274.

Guba, E. G., and Lincoln, Y. S. "Do Inquiry Paradigms Imply Inquiry Methodologies?" In D. M. Fetterman (ed.), *Qualitative Approaches to Evaluation in Education.* New York: Praeger, 1988.

Guba, E. G., and Lincoln, Y. S. *Fourth Generation Evaluation.* Thousand Oaks, Calif.: Sage, 1989.

Guba, E. G., and Lincoln, Y. S. "Competing Paradigms in Qualitative Research." In N. K. Denzin and Y. S. Lincoln (eds.), *Handbook of Qualitative Research.* Thousand Oaks, Calif.: Sage, 1994.

Gunn, D. S., and Sanford, T. R. "Doctoral Student Retention." *College and University,* 1988, *63,* 374–382.

Hale, W. G. "The Doctor's Dissertation." In *The Association of American Universities: Papers and Discussions During the Third Annual Conference.* Chicago: Association of American Universities, Feb. 25–27, 1902.

Hall, G. S. "University Research." *Pedagogical Seminary,* 1916, *23,* 97–113.

Hammersley, M., and Atkinson, P. *Ethnography: Principles in Practice.* (2nd ed.) New York: Routledge, 1995.

Hanson, T. L. "The ABD Phenomenon: The 'at Risk' Population in Higher Education and the Discipline of Communication." Paper presented at the annual meeting of the Speech Communication Association, Chicago, Oct. 1992.

Hatley, R. V., and Fiene, J. R. "Enhancing Doctoral Student Progress and Improving Dissertation Quality: A Success Scenario." Paper presented at the annual meeting of the American Educational Research Association, San Francisco, Apr. 1995.

Hawkins, H. *Pioneer: A History of the Johns Hopkins University, 1874–1889.* Ithaca, N.Y.: Cornell University Press, 1960.

Hawkins, H. *Banding Together: The Rise of National Associations in American Higher Education, 1887–1950.* Baltimore: Johns Hopkins University Press, 1992.

Haworth, J. G. "Doctoral Programs in American Higher Education." In J. C. Smart (ed.), *Higher Education: Handbook of Theory and Research.* Vol. 11. New York: Agathon Press, 1996.

Heinrich, K. T. "Loving Partnerships: Dealing with Sexual Attraction and Power in Doctoral Advisement Relationships." *Journal of Higher Education,* 1991, *62,* 514–538.

Heinrich, K. T. "Doctoral Advisement Relationships: On Friendship and Betrayal." *Journal of Higher Education,* 1995, *66,* 447–469.

Heiss, A. M. *Challenges to Graduate Schools.* San Francisco: Jossey-Bass, 1970.

Hendlin, S. J. *When Good Enough Is Never Enough: Escaping the Perfection Trap.* New York: Putnam, 1992.

Herbst, J. *The German Historical School in American Scholarship: A Study in the Transfer of Culture.* Ithaca, N.Y.: Cornell University Press, 1965.

Hill, M. B., Hill, D. A., Chabot, A. E., and Barrall, J. R. "A Survey of College Faculty and Student Procrastination." *College Student Journal,* 1978, *12,* 256–262.

Hobish, T. T. "A Study of Selected Psychological Factors Related to Completion or Non-Completion of the Doctoral Dissertation Among Male and Female Doctoral Degree Candidates." Ph.D. diss., New York University, 1978. Abstract in *Dissertational Abstracts International,* 1978, *39,* 1934B.

Holden, C. "Careers '95: The Future of the Ph.D." *Science,* 1995, *270* (6), 121–146.

Huguley, S. "An Investigation of Obstacles to Completion of the Dissertation and of Doctoral Student Attitudes Toward Dissertation Experience." Ph.D. diss., Pepperdine University, 1988. Abstract in *Dissertation Abstracts International,* 1989, *50* (2), 372A.

Isaac, P. D., Quinlan, S. V., and Walker, M. M. "Faculty Perceptions of the Doctoral Dissertation." *Journal of Higher Education,* 1992, *63,* 241–268.

Johns Hopkins Library. *List of Dissertations . . . 1876–1926.* Baltimore: Johns Hopkins University Press, 1926.

Johns Hopkins University Register. FHA, Johns Hopkins University, 1877–1878.

Johnson, J., and Bloom, M. "Procrastination and the Five-Factor Theory of Personality." Paper presented at the meeting of the Society for the Study of Individual Differences, Baltimore, July 1993.

Jungnickel, P. "Workplace Correlates and Scholarly Performance of Pharmacy Clinical Faculty Members." Ph.D. diss., University of Nebraska, Lincoln, 1993. Abstract in *Dissertation Abstracts International,* 1994, *55* (01), 49A.

Katz, E., Green, K. E., Kluever, R., Lenz, K., and Miller, M. "Graduates and ABDs in Colleges of Education: Characteristics and Implications for the Structure of Doctoral Programs." A symposium presented at the annual meeting of the American Educational Research Association, San Francisco, Apr. 1995. (ED 382 143)

Katz, J. "Development of the Mind." In J. Katz and R. T. Hartnett (eds.), *Scholars in the Making.* New York: Ballinger, 1976.

Kindleberger, C. P. *The Life of an Economist: An Autobiography.* Cambridge, Mass.: Blackwell, 1991.

Koelsch, W. A. *Clark University, 1887–1987: A Narrative History.* Worcester, Mass.: Clark University Press, 1987.

Krathwohl, D. R. *Social and Behavioral Science Research.* San Francisco: Jossey-Bass, 1987.

Krueger, R. A. *Focus Groups: A Practical Guide for Applied Research.* (2nd ed.) Thousand Oaks, Calif.: Sage, 1994.

Lenz, K. S. "A Multiple Case Study Examining Factors Affecting the Completion of the Doctoral Dissertation by Academically Able Women." Ph.D. diss., University of Denver, 1994. Abstract in *Dissertation Abstracts International,* 1994, *55* (12), 3714A.

"Letters." *New York Times Magazine,* Oct. 13, 1996, pp. 16–18.

Lipschutz, S. S. "Enhancing Success in Doctoral Education: From Policy to Practice." In L. L. Baird (ed.), *Increasing Graduate Student Retention and Degree Attainment.* San Francisco: Jossey-Bass, 1993.

Locke, L. F., Spirduso, W. W., and Silverman, S. J. *Proposals That Work: A Guide for Planning Dissertations and Grant Proposals.* Thousand Oaks, Calif.: Sage, 1987.

Lozoff, M. M. "Interpersonal Relations and Autonomy." In J. Katz and R. T. Hartnett (eds.), *Scholars in the Making.* New York: Ballinger, 1976.

Madsen, D. *Successful Dissertations and Theses: A Guide to Graduate Student Research from Proposal to Completion.* (2nd ed.) San Francisco: Jossey-Bass, 1992.

Magner, D. K. "More Black Ph.D.'s." *Chronicle of Higher Education,* 1996, *42,* A25–A26.

Marsden, G. M. *The Soul of the American University: From Protestant Establishment to Established Nonbelief.* New York: Oxford University Press, 1994.

Marshall, C., and Rossman, G. B. *Designing Qualitative Research.* (2nd ed.) Thousand Oaks, Calif.: Sage, 1995.

Maxwell, J. *Qualitative Research Design: An Interactive Approach.* Thousand Oaks, Calif.: Sage, 1996.

Mayhew, L. B. *Reform in Graduate Education.* Southern Regional Education Board Monograph no. 18, Atlanta, 1972.

McCown, W., Petzel, T., and Rupert, P. "Personality Correlates and Behaviors of Chronic Procrastinators." *Personality and Individual Differences,* 1987, *11,* 71–79.

McKean, K. J. "An Investigation of Academic Procrastination as a Behavioral Manifestation of Learned Helplessness." Ph.D. diss., Seton Hall University, 1990. Abstract in *Dissertational Abstracts International,* 1990, *51* (11), 5581B.

Menand, L. "How to Make a Ph.D. Matter." *New York Times Magazine,* Sept. 22, 1996, pp. 78–81.

Merriam, S. "Mentors and Protégés: A Critical Review of the Literature." *Adult Education Quarterly,* 1983, *33,* 161–173.

Milgram, N. A., Batori, G., and Mowrer, D. "Correlates of Academic Procrastination." *Journal of School Psychology,* 1993, *31,* 487–500.

Miller, D. C. *Handbook of Research Design and Social Measurement.* (5th ed.) Thousand Oaks, Calif.: Sage, 1991.

Miller, J. *Toward a New Psychology of Women.* Boston: Beacon Press, 1976.

Miselis, K. L., McManus, W., and Kraus, E. "We Can Improve Our Graduate Programs: Analysis of Ph.D. Student Attrition and Time-to-Degree at the University of Pennsylvania." Paper presented at the annual forum of the Association of Institutional Research, San Francisco, May 1991.

Morrow, R. A., and Brown, D. D. *Critical Theory and Methodology.* Thousand Oaks, Calif.: Sage, 1994.

Moustakas, C. *Phenomenological Research Methods.* Thousand Oaks, Calif.: Sage, 1994.

Muszynski, S. Y., and Akamatsu, T. J. "Delay in Completion of Doctoral Dissertations in Clinical Psychology." *Professional Psychology: Research and Practice,* 1991, *22,* 119–123.

National Research Council. Ad Hoc Panel on Graduate Attrition, Office of Scientific and Engineering Personnel. *The Path to the Ph.D.: Measuring Graduate Attrition in the Sciences and Humanities.* Washington, D.C.: National Academy Press, 1996.

National Research Council. Committee for the Study of Research-Doctorate Programs in the United States. *Research-Doctorate Programs in the United States: Continuity and Change.* Washington, D.C.: National Academy Press, 1995.

National Science Foundation. *NSF Special Report no. 92–332.* Washington, D.C.: National Science Foundation, 1992.

National Science Foundation. "Women, Minorities, and Persons with Disabilities in Science and Engineering." In *NSF Report no. 96–311.* Washington, D.C.: National Science Foundation, 1996.

Nerad, M. "Doctoral Education at the University of California and Factors Affecting Time-to-Degree." Unpublished report, Office of the President, University of California, 1991.

Nerad, M., and Cerny, J. "From Facts to Action: Expanding the Educational Role of the Graduate Division." In L. L. Baird (ed.), *Increasing Graduate Student Retention and Degree Attainment.* San Francisco: Jossey-Bass, 1993. First published in *Council of Graduate Schools Communicator* (Washington, D.C.: Council of Graduate Schools, 1991).

Noble, K. A. *Changing Doctoral Degrees: An International Perspective.* Buckingham, England: Society for Research into Higher Education; Open University Press, 1994.

Nuesse, C. J. *The Catholic University of America: A Centennial History.* Washington, D.C.: Catholic University of America Press, 1990.

Pelikan, J. *Scholarship and Its Survival: Questions on the Idea of Graduate Education.* Princeton, N.J.: Princeton University Press, 1983.

Reichardt, C., and Rallis, S. F. *The Quantitative and Qualitative Debate: New Perspectives.* San Francisco: Jossey-Bass, 1994.

Reinharz, S. *Feminist Methods in Social Research.* Oxford, England: Oxford University Press, 1992.

Rennie, D. L., and Brewer, L. "A Grounded Theory of Thesis Blocking." *Teaching of Psychology,* 1987, *14,* 10–16.

Ries, P., and Thurgood, D. H. *Summary Report 1992: Doctorate Recipients from United States Universities.* Washington, D.C.: National Academy Press, 1993.

Roberts, S. M., Fulton, M., and Semb, G. "Self-Pacing in a Personalized Psychology Course: Letting Students Set the Deadlines." *Teaching of Psychology,* 1988, *15,* 89–92.

Rosenblatt, S. *The Days of My Years: An Autobiography.* Hoboken, N.J.: Ktav, 1976.

Rothblum, E. D., Solomon, L. J., and Murakami, J. "Affective, Cognitive, and Behavioral Differences Between High and Low Procrastinators." *Journal of Counseling Psychology,* 1986, *33,* 387–394.

Ryan, W. C. *Studies in Early Graduate Education: The Johns Hopkins, Clark University, the University of Chicago.* Bulletin no. 30. New York: Carnegie Foundation for the Advancement of Teaching, 1939.

Saddler, D. C., and Sacks, L. A. "Multidimensional Perfectionism and Academic Procrastination: Relationships with Depression in University Students." *Psychological Reports,* 1993, 73, 863–871.

Sands, R. G., Parson, L. A., and Duane, J. "Faculty Mentoring Faculty in a Public University." *Journal of Higher Education,* 1991, 62, 184–193.

Schlesinger, A. M. *In Retrospect: The History of a Historian.* Orlando, Fla.: Harcourt Brace, 1963.

Semrow, J. J., Barney, J. A., Fredericks, J., Fredericks, M., Robinson, BVM, P., and Pfnister, A. O. *In Search of Quality: The Development, Status, and Forecast of Standards in Postsecondary Accreditation.* New York: Lang, 1992.

Skelly, M. E. "There's No Quick-Fix for the Ph.D. Shortage." *School and College,* 1990, 90, 13–16.

Sloan, D. *The Scottish Enlightenment and the American College Ideal.* New York: Teachers College Press, 1971.

Smith, J. M. "Completing the Doctoral Dissertation in Clinical Psychology." Ph.D. diss., Adelphi University, 1985. Abstract in *Dissertation Abstracts International,* 1985, 46, 662B.

Snell, J. L. *The Education of Historians in the United States.* New York: McGraw-Hill, 1963.

Solomon, L. J., and Rothblum, E. D. "Academic Procrastination: Frequency and Cognitive-Behavioral Correlates." *Journal of Counseling Psychology,* 1984, 31, 503–509.

Sparkes, A. C. "The Paradigms Debate: An Extended Review and a Celebration of Difference." In A. C. Sparkes (ed.), *Research in Physical Education and Sport: Exploring Alternative Visions.* Bristol, Pa.: Falmer Press, 1992.

Stake, R. *The Art of Case Study Research.* Thousand Oaks, Calif.: Sage, 1995.

Stein, E., and Weidman, J. "The Socialization of Doctoral Students to Academic Norms." Paper presented at the annual meeting of the American Educational Research Association, Boston, Apr. 1990.

Stern, F. P. "The Effects of Separation-Individuation Conflicts on Length of Time to Complete the Dissertation." Ph.D. diss., City University of New York, 1985. Abstract in *Dissertation Abstracts International,* 1985, 46 (11), 4030B.

Sternberg, D. *How to Complete and Survive a Doctoral Dissertation.* New York: St. Martin's Press, 1981.

Stewart, A. J. "Toward a Feminist Strategy for Studying Women's Lives." In C. E. Franz and A. J. Stewart (eds.), *Women Creating Lives: Identities, Resilience, and Resistance.* Boulder, Colo.: Westview Press, 1994.

Storr, R. J. *The Beginnings of Graduate Education in America.* Chicago: University of Chicago Press, 1953.

Storr, R. J. *The Beginning of the Future: A Historical Approach to Graduate Education in the Arts and Sciences.* Carnegie Commission on Higher Education. New York: McGraw-Hill, 1973.

Strauss, A., and Corbin, J. *Basics of Qualitative Research: Grounded Theory Procedures and Techniques.* Thousand Oaks, Calif.: Sage, 1990.

Surrey, J. L. "The 'Self-in-Relation' Theory: A Theory of Women's Development." In J. V. Jordan, A. G. Kaplan, J. Baker Miller, I. P. Stiver, and J. L. Surrey (eds.), *Women's Growth in Connection.* New York: Guilford Press, 1991.

Szanton, D. "Interdisciplinary Communities for Dissertation Writers." *Chronicle of Higher Education,* Feb. 23, 1994, B3.

Taylor, R. R. "Procrastination: The Personality and Situational Correlates of Procrastination Behavior for Achievement Tasks." Ph.D. diss., Louisiana State University, 1979. Abstract in *Dissertation Abstracts International,* 1979, 40 (04), 1967B.

Tesch, R. *Qualitative Research: Analysis Types and Software Tools.* Bristol, Pa.: Falmer Press, 1990.

Thomas, C. C. "On-Line to Advanced Degrees." *Graduating Engineer,* 1996, 17 (2), 36–37.

Thomas, C. C. "The Twenty-First Century Engineer." *Graduating Engineer,* 1997, *18* (3), 24–26.

Tierney, W. G., and Rhoads, R. A. *Faculty Socialization as a Cultural Process: A Mirror of Institutional Commitment.* ASHE-ERIC Higher Education Report no. 6. Washington, D.C.: George Washington University and the Association for the Study of Higher Education, 1993.

Tinto, V. *Leaving College: Rethinking the Causes and Cures of Student Attrition.* Chicago: University of Chicago Press, 1987.

Tinto, V. "Toward a Theory of Doctoral Persistence." Paper presented at the annual meeting of the American Educational Research Association, Chicago, Apr. 1991.

Trow, M. "Federalism in American Higher Education." In A. Levine (ed.), *Higher Learning in America, 1980–2000.* Baltimore: Johns Hopkins University Press, 1993.

Tuckman, H., Coyle, S., and Bae, Y. *On Time to the Doctorate.* Washington, D.C.: National Academy Press, 1990.

Turner, J., and Bernard, P. "The Prussian Road to University? German Models and the University of Michigan, 1837–c. 1895." In *Fifty Years: Horace H. Rackham School of Graduate Studies, 1988–1989.* Ann Arbor: University of Michigan, 1989.

University of Chicago Announcements. *Doctors of Philosophy, June 1893–Apr. 1931, Register Number.* Vol. 31, no. 19. Chicago: University of Chicago Press, 1931.

Veysey, L. R. *The Emergence of the American University.* Chicago: University of Chicago Press, 1965.

Wagner, D. V. "Selected Personality Characteristics and Situational Factors as Correlates of Completion and Non-Completion of the Doctoral Dissertation." Ph.D. diss., University of Michigan, 1986. Abstract in *Dissertation Abstracts International,* 1986, *47,* 3377A.

Washington, C. "Where Science and Engineering Ph.D.s Get Their B.A.s." *Higher Education and National Affairs,* 1993, *42* (14), 3.

Webster, D. S., and Skinner, T. "Rating Ph.D. Programs: What the NCR Report Says . . . and Doesn't Say." *Change,* 1996, *28* (3), 22–44.

Weil, R. L. "Factors Affecting Doctoral Students' Time to Degree." Ph.D. diss., Claremont Graduate School, 1988. Abstract in *Dissertation Abstracts International,* 1988, *51* (04), 1138A.

Weiss, L. "The Relationship Between Personality Variables and Completion of a Doctoral Dissertation." Ph.D. diss., California School of Professional Psychology, 1987. Abstract in *Dissertation Abstracts International,* 1987, *48* (09), 3814A–3815A.

Wentzel, M. L. "The Relationship of Locus of Control Orientation to the Academic Achievement of Doctoral Students." Ph.D. diss., North Texas State University, 1987. Abstract in *Dissertation Abstracts International,* 1987, *48* (03), 615A.

White, J. W. "Graduate Instruction in the United States." In B. W. Bradley (ed.), *The Graduate Handbook, no. 7, 1899.* Philadelphia: Lippincott, 1899.

Williams, R. L. *The Origins of Federal Support for Higher Education: George W. Atherton and the Land-Grant College Movement.* University Park, Pa.: Pennsylvania State University Press, 1991.

Willis, P. *Learning to Labour: How Working Class Kids Get Working Class Jobs.* Westmead, England: Saxon House, 1977.

Wilson, K. M. *Of Time and the Doctorate: Report of an Inquiry into the Duration of Doctoral Study.* Atlanta: Southern Regional Education Board, 1965.

Wilson, W. *The Papers of Woodrow Wilson.* 4 vols. Edited by A. S. Link. Princeton, N.J.: Princeton University Press, 1966.

Wolcott, H. F. "On Seeking—and Rejecting—Validity in Qualitative Research." In E. W. Eisner and A. Peshkin (eds.), *Qualitative Inquiry in Education.* New York: Teachers College Press, 1990.

Wright, L. M. "Full Time Teaching and the ABD Phenomenon." *American Communication Association Bulletin,* 1991, *76,* 49–53.

Ziolkowski, T. "The Ph.D. Squid." *American Scholar,* 1990, *59,* 175–195.

INDEX

Campus residency/proximity, and dissertation completion, 10, 50, 52, 55

Candidates. *See* Students, "All But Dissertation" (ABD); Students, doctoral

Caracelli, V. J., 46

Carmichael, O. C., 14

Carnegie Corporation, 31

Carnegie Foundation for the Advancement of Teaching, 17, 28, 32

Case study approach, 43

Catholic University of America, 27; early doctoral programs at, 21–22

Cerny, J., 5, 15, 80

Cesari, J. P., 47

Chabot, A. E., 59

Challenges to Graduate Schools (Heiss), 31

Childhood loss, 58

Chodorow, N., 67

Chronicle of Higher Education, 1

Clark University, 27, 28; Carnegie study of, 28; doctoral productivity at, 1878–1918, 24–26; early doctoral programs at, 21, 23–24; G. Stanley Hall at, 23, 24, 26, 27, 28

Clifford, G. J., 7

Cognitive ecology, 13

Columbia University, 27; early doctoral programs at, 21, 29

Cone, J. D., 6, 13

Conference Board of Associated Research Councils, 32

Conformance, achievement via, 58

Constitutional Convention, 1787, 18

Constructionist approach, 33. *See also* Interpretive research methodologies

Control, locus of, 58, 63–64

Corbin, J., 37, 43

Cordasco, F., 17, 20–21, 23

Cornell University, 27

Council of Graduate Schools, 5, 6, 7, 15, 76–77, 99, 101

Course selection: for ideological research methodologies, 42, 44; impact of research methodologies on, 33, 41–46, 102; for interpretive research methodologies, 42, 43–44; for positivist research methodologies, 41, 42; for pragmatic research methodologies, 42, 45

Coyle, S., 100

Creswell, J. W., 33, 34, 36, 37–38, 39, 40, 43, 44, 45, 46, 102

Critical theory research, 34, 38, 39. *See also* Ideological research methodologies

Cultural perspectives, 38. *See also* Ideological research methodologies

Cunningham, J. W., 34, 35

Dana, J. D., 20, 23

Davis, G. B., 11

Denzin, N. K., 43

Dependency needs, 58, 60, 63–64

Diamond, 2

Dickens, C. S., 36, 39

Digest of Education Statistics (U.S. Department of Education), 17, 65, 66

"Directory of Engineering Employment," 94–95

Disabilities, persons with, 92. *See also* Minorities

Dissertation committee: choosing members for, 102; student relationship with, 86–87; support from, 50, 53, 56. *See also* Faculty affiliation

Dissertation completion, 99–105; ABD student perspectives on, 47–56; factors in, 5, 6, 8–9, 10–11, 47–56, 57–64, 100–101; factors in, for nontraditional-aged women, 65–74; graduate student perspectives on, 47–56; nexus of responsibility for, 105; psychosocial factors affecting, 57–64; rates of, 2, 5, 47, 57; recommendations for, 73–74; student employment impact on, 49–50; studies of, 100–101; tasks for facilitating, 52; and university size, 72–73; university support for, 75–89; of women, 9, 65–74. *See also* Adviser-student relationship; Advisers; Control, locus of; Dependency needs; Doctoral completion; Emotional support; Family support; Financial support; Peer support; Perfectionism; Persistence; Procrastination; Research experience; Support

Dissertation Day, 15

Dissertation defense, 13

Dissertation process, 5–16; adviser's role in, 7, 15, 56, 102; AAU discussion of, 1902, 28; arguments for and against, 1–2; elements of, 101–104; emergence of, in first research universities, 21–26; faculty roles in, 104; guidance sources for, 102–103; historical development of, 17–32, 75–76; idea element of, 102; key players in, 7; as obstacle to doctoral completion, 6–7, 10–11, 99; and professionalization of faculty, 2; program roles in, 104; purposes of, 6; recommendations for improving, 13–15; research methodologies and, 33–46, 102; society's

ORDERING INFORMATION

NEW DIRECTIONS FOR HIGHER EDUCATION is a series of paperback books that provides timely information and authoritative advice about major issues and administrative problems confronting every institution. Books in the series are published quarterly in Spring, Summer, Fall, and Winter and are available for purchase by subscription and individually.

SUBSCRIPTIONS cost $54.00 for individuals (a savings of 35 percent over single-copy prices) and $90.00 for institutions, agencies, and libraries. Standing orders are accepted. New York residents, add local tax for subscriptions. (For subscriptions outside the United States, add $7.00 for shipping via surface mail or $25.00 for air mail. Orders *must be prepaid* in U.S. dollars by check drawn on a U.S. bank or charged to VISA, MasterCard, or American Express.)

SINGLE COPIES cost $22.00 plus shipping (see below) when payment accompanies order. California, New Jersey, New York, and Washington, D.C., residents, please include appropriate sales tax. Canadian residents, add GST and any local taxes. Billed orders will be charged shipping and handling. No billed shipments to post office boxes. (Orders from outside the United States *must be prepaid* in U.S. dollars by check drawn on a U.S. bank or charged to VISA, MasterCard, or American Express.)

SHIPPING (SINGLE COPIES ONLY): $30.00 and under, add $5.50; to $50.00, add $6.50; to $75.00, add $7.50; to $100.00, add $9.00; to $150.00, add $10.00.

ALL PRICES are subject to change.

DISCOUNTS FOR QUANTITY ORDERS are available. Please write to the address below for information.

ALL ORDERS must include either the name of an individual or an official purchase order number. Please submit your order as follows:
   Subscriptions: specify series and year subscription is to begin
   Single copies: include individual title code (such as HE82)

MAIL ALL ORDERS TO:
   Jossey-Bass Publishers
   350 Sansome Street
   San Francisco, California 94104-1342

PHONE subscription or single-copy orders toll-free at (888) 378-2537 or at (415) 433-1767 (toll call).

FAX orders toll-free to: (800) 605-2665

FOR SUBSCRIPTION SALES OUTSIDE OF THE UNITED STATES, contact any international subscription agency or Jossey-Bass directly.